MW01602669

BEST POETS OF 2024

VOL. 2

John T. Eber Sr.
MANAGING EDITOR

A publication of

Eber & Wein Publishing

Pennsylvania

Best Poets of 2024: Vol. 2
Copyright © 2025 by Eber & Wein Publishing as a compilation.

Library of Congress
Cataloging in Publication Data

ISBN 978-1-60880-798-7

Proudly manufactured in the United States of America by

Eber & Wein Publishing
Pennsylvania

A Note from the Editor . . .

Poetry has long been a vessel for human expression, a way to capture fleeting emotions, profound experiences, and the very essence of what it means to be alive. Yet, in an age dominated by digital noise, the relevance of poetry often comes into question. Still, poetry persists—not just through the celebrated works of literary giants, but through the voices of amateur poets who keep the art form alive in everyday spaces.

Amateur poets are the heart of poetry's continued relevance. You remind us that poetry is not confined to academia or the pages of prestigious journals; it thrives in handwritten notebooks, spoken-word performances, and even social media posts. Amateur poets play a vital role in keeping poetry alive because they write not for accolades but for expression. A mother jotting down a few lines about her child's laughter, a student scribbling verses in the margins of their notebook, or a worker capturing the monotony and necessity of daily labor—these voices form the heart of modern poetry. You write because you need to, because emotions are too profound to be kept inside, and because poetry allows you to make sense of your world. Poetry's accessibility allows anyone to engage with it, to shape their world through words, and to share their unique perspectives with others. Whether penned in solitude or performed on a stage, poetry remains a deeply personal yet universally resonant art.

So why do people, regardless of background, turn to poetry? The answer lies in poetry's ability to distill emotions into their purest form. It provides a space for introspection, catharsis, and connection. A poem can be a moment of stillness in a chaotic world, a way to process grief, love, wonder, or longing. It offers both writer and reader a sense of belonging—an understanding that someone else, somewhere, has felt the same.

At its core, poetry is an invocation of imagination. Figments of love, emotion, imagination, and the soul transform into poetry through the alchemy of language—where raw feelings, fleeting thoughts, and intangible experiences find shape, rhythm, and resonance. Poetry acts as a bridge between the unseen and the written word, turning internal landscapes into something others can feel, understand, and connect with. Sometimes, a poem begins with just a single figment that lingers in the mind, refusing to be ignored. Other times, it is sparked by a dream, a memory, or an observation that transforms into something greater than itself.

Poetry invites the unreal, the metaphorical, and the abstract into our consciousness, allowing us to see the world anew. As long as people feel, dream, and imagine, poetry will remain relevant. And as long as there are voices willing to speak, poetry will never be silent.

June 2024 first place winner Danny Brookhart draws poetic inspiration from Charles Dickens' classic novel *Great Expectations,* cleverly illustrating a modern, surreal reimagining of Miss Havisham's character and the purposeful, merciless, emotional pain she inflicts upon Pip. Through its vivid imagery and eerie tone, it reflects key aspects of the novel—particularly loss, decay, stagnation of time, and emotional paralysis.

By placing her in a modern setting—Joe's bar—the poem emphasizes that Miss Havisham's sorrow and haunting presence transcend time, much like how her emotional wounds never truly heal in the novel. The stopping of the clock at twenty to nine is a direct connection to Miss Havisham's clock, which remains frozen at the moment she was abandoned at the altar. This symbol of time's suspension underscores how she is emotionally trapped in that painful moment, unable to move forward. Similarly, the speaker of the poem also appears stuck in time in their own sorrow, paralleling Miss Havisham's arrested emotional state.

Her physical depiction is unsettling—"Bony fingers," "broken nails," and a "crumpled old piece of paper"—suggesting she is a relic of the past, much like the original character in her ruined mansion. The poem adds an unusual modern twist with "Christian Dior," contrasting contemporary luxury with her decayed state, much like how Miss Havisham's wealth exists in stark contrast to her personal ruin.

The interaction between the speaker and the woman is ambiguous, much like Pip's uneasy encounters with Miss Havisham in the novel. Her "hiss through clenched teeth" and the symbolic act of handing him a pencil create a sense of mystery. The pencil could represent the potential to rewrite the past—an opportunity that neither Miss Havisham nor Pip truly receives in *Great Expectations*—or change fate and move aside the empty glass, symbolic of an empty future devoid of love.

This poem captures the essence of Miss Havisham's ghostly presence and the lasting impact of lost love, while also drawing strong parallels to Pip's emotional journey. The stopped clock, the decayed wedding attire, the theme of regret, and the symbolic question of loss all serve as echoes of Dickens' novel, transporting its themes into a contemporary yet timeless setting. Much like the novel, the poem explores the consequences of dwelling in the past and the haunting nature of unresolved, all-consuming grief.

Amber Pease
Editor

Havisham Time

I remember that night when she walked into Joe's.
At that time of year,
the clock stopped at twenty-to-nine, just like my heart.

All tightly wrapped in what remained of a wedding dress,
yellow stained silk and lace,
it had a tattered veil hanging out of her greying, matted hair.

She had an odd walk, and I was sure she lost a shoe along the way.
Bony fingers pointed around the bar, covered with
tarnished jewelry and ending in broken nails.
She had a crumpled old piece of paper clutched in her hand,
and I could tell she was all business.

When she passed my steel barstool,
I caught a whiff of something,
and it wasn't Christian Dior.

She dragged a stool beside me, and the bartender, Arthur,
asked if she wanted something.
She just hissed at him through clenched teeth.

Then she leaned in close to me and whispered,
"Do you feel like you have lost her?"
She placed a pencil on the bar in front of me.
And all I could do was stare into my empty glass.

Danny Brookhart
Scottsdale, AZ

If I Could Only See You Again

If I could only see you again,
how happy I would be

Just to see your smiling face, to tell you
how much I love you

I want to tell you how much I miss you,
how much I miss your hugs, your kisses,
and how much I need you

Words could never express the pain that
I feel in my heart

If I could turn back the hands of
time, you would still be here with me

Sometimes when I hear some of our old
songs on the radio, it brings tears to
my eyes, thinking about all of the wonderful
times we had together

Now, I'm alone without you with all of
the wonderful memories of you; of which
is all I have that will last me a lifetime

I thank God for the time we had
together, for I will love you *always*!

Roseztta Summers
Saint George, SC

For the Thrill

Have you ever felt what it feels like to fly?
Felt the air rushing around you
The bugs hitting you everywhere
The smell of the trees on the air
Each breath awakening a memory
The land rushing past you in a swirl of colors
To me, this is what it feels like to be alive
A promise of freedom
All stress gone, all negative thoughts forgotten
Only the now remaining
The feel of the engine rumbling underneath
This is bliss, a sudden rush of adrenaline
This is my happiness
Those who have never ridden a motorcycle
Would never understand this feeling of freedom
It is a whole different world
A wondrous experience
And yet it is so terrifying and surreal
Knowing that any moment it all could be taken away
A single blink and it's all gone
We do it for fun, for the thrill
Hearts racing and smiles upon us
We forget all else and become one with the machine

Brittany Sarkozi
New Boston, MI

Waves

My grief has become a tide.
Glimpses of you flash, dismantling real from fake.
I wish you wouldn't have died.

The seven years we had was a difficult ride,
like an ever growing tree that would not break.
My grief has become a tide.

I feel guilty on days I haven't cried.
A year has come, and I'm still at your wake.
I wish you wouldn't have died.

So many days I should've swallowed my pride,
avoiding this heart-crushing ache.
My grief has become a tide.

So many times I tried
to stop your morbid mistake.
I wish you wouldn't have died.

You broke me with your suicide.
Now when I sleep, I'm awake.
My grief has become a tide.
I wish you wouldn't have died.

Kourtney Marie Birdsall
Gurnee, IL

I was previously published in Endless Horizons back in 2009 after receiving my bachelor's degree. Since then, I have earned my master's degree in professional writing and rhetoric, gotten married, had two daughters, taught English composition I and II at my alma mater, University of Wisconsin-Parkside, and worked in various fields in the writing industry. This poem was inspired by the grief I felt after the suicide of my ex-fiance, whose death ultimately inspired me to go on in my education and earn my master's degree as well as study psychology and writing, using writing as a form of catharsis for healing.

20 Years Later

Orlando, Florida, 2005, straight out of foster care
Go off to the university without a scare
You'll be a high school track star
On a collegiate scholarship to run far
Don't party all your tuition away
To then Marry Jane on the runway
Don't drop out of college
Be incarcerated and throw away international knowledge
Then wonder why you couldn't pay the rent
Because your pipe dreams were too exhausted to vent
Leave Babson Park's orange groves for the big city
To Tampa, Florida in search of opportunity, not pity
Then sleep on your cousin's couch
When life (truly) hits you, ouch
Join the military
The unknown will have more curiosity than scary
Be single, married, deployed, and then divorced
Don't chase a childhood void when its forced
Tell yourself to finish your degree
Become an officer and your future family trustee
Then travel to 25 countries on 5 continents overseas
Around the Earth on jets, summer water and winter skis
Buy a house, happily married, with a wife and four kids
Earn a master's degree, work on Capitol Hill, shut lids
Your kids will have loving parents, don't be a hater
And this is where you'll see yourself 20 years later!

Artist Clay Jones
Fort Belvoir, VA

This is my 15th published poem with Eber & Wein! Special thanks to Cousin Rodney and Uncle Ernest Jones, "Love You Forever!" Huge thanks Sarah-Jane Turner, Kathy Kenney, Carlos Guerrero, Abigail Cranor, Nicole Jamieson, Patrick Spence, Elisa Castro-Leyva, Shawn Gutierrez, Nicoloe Alexander, Sam Hancock, Samuel Robinson, Michael Carson, Leslie Shipp, Peter Hebert, Jane Peacock, Marcus Ellerbe, Monica Patton-Neal, Al Cooper, Ebony Thomas, Heidi Hoyle and families: Notaro, Papp, Reillo, Linson, Guinta, Murphy, Boetner, Pasciuta, Seward, Jones! Supreme Thanks to my gorgeous wife, LoveLeigh, and my beautiful and brilliant children, Artist II, Aquarian, LoveLeiella, ArtLovian! "Love You Five Forever!"

Walked

Warriors, prophets, young men and women—all the people who have
walked the earth leaving their mark on it whether for good or evil.
Where are the leaders we are withering away
for lack of purpose and direction.
Promises from men and women are shallow and hollow,
no real meaning just empty words.
Their souls have no fire for justice.

Patricia Sandraco
Round Lake Beach, IL

I love to express my feelings in poetry. I want more than anything for peace.

One Wish

If I had but one wish
I would not wish for gold
If I had but one wish
I would not wish for fame
If I had but one wish
I would not wish for glory
If I had but one wish
I would wish for just a moment reset
A moment to take back my words
A moment to heal
If I had but one wish
A wish for just a moment reset

Joy Everett
Alvin, TX

The Winter View

The winter wind is blowing;
You can hear it howling,
As heavy snowflakes are falling.

The sun is playing peek-a-boo,
As the clouds play Guess Who?
And they are as gray as Eeyore in Winnie the Pooh.

The trees are clothed with beautiful gowns;
Icicles are forming as they drop down,
With a white sparkling blanket covering the ground.

The temperature is brutal out;
It's minus zero without a doubt!
That nothing wants to take route.

This marvelous view is glowing.
It's a picture well worth seeing;
Only God could create what is displaying.

I am thankful as I look outside
For this view and my fireplace blazing with pride,
As I stay warm sipping on my coffee here inside.

Audra J. Walls
Lima, OH

I am a legally-blind, partly-deaf woman who loves the Lord, poetry, and life. It is not easy for me to read or write; it takes me more time because I have to look to the right of the word before reading. Spelling is also difficult for me; it is by the grace of God that I can read and write, plus the patience of my mother, who spent countless hours helping me learn. My reason for writing comes from my Lord and Savior Jesus Christ; it is a gift He has given me.

Mom's Cry

As I wipe the tears out of my eyes

From the loss of a daughter, who
shut the door of her life
away from me.

Who will not let me see her face
or listen to her voice.
Saying hello mom, to me.

Why must this be, my heart cries?
How can unknown angry or
problems divide?

Doesn't she know love is more than
all she thinks in her heart?

Push away those fears, oh girl,
I love so much.

Open to the light of hope and a
changed decision.

Be whole in your heart,
come let us speak and reason.

Let us close our lives in a healed
love, not our pride.

Yvonne Jo Queen
Oneco, FL

Rejoice

Beauty of nature calls
With the echo of the wind
Leaves blowing gently
On the ground
Sunshine to light our way

Sounds of birds singing
Rejoice, rejoice, it's another day
God's voice can be heard
In every mountaintop
Every sound of nature

Fluttering of a butterfly's wings
A rainbow to brighten our day
Peace fills my soul
Every breath of life
A newborn baby's first cry

Blossoming of flowers
Orange, pink, yellow, blue, lavender so true
Showing God's great love
For you
I say, *Rejoice!*

Laura Jean M. Barbato
Wooster, OH

My Sweet Peter

My heart belongs to
you, my sweet Peter.
You are my one true
love. The only love
I have ever had is
for you and always
will. No one else I
will ever love except
my sweet Peter,
now and forever.

Elizabeth A. Anzalone
South Plainfield, NJ

Little Girls

Little girls with blonde, dark, or red hair
Little girls wearing scraggly ribbons or hair clips
Little girls with light or dark skin tones
Little girls pretending to be nurses or doctors
Superintendents or teachers
Mechanics, firefighters, or policewomen
Little girls acting like tomboys; little girls being girly
Little girls crying and giggling about nothing
Little girls offering sympathy to depressed adults
God bless little girls!

Marian Louise Malone
Lincoln, NE

A Check Up

I went to the doctor one day
and they said I was sick in
some sort of way. I said
how could that be, I'm
very healthy as you can
see, a health physical went
very well indeed. One nurse
said, you have the blood we
need, so they did a surgery
on me indeed, made me
weak for no one's needs.
My name the same, it
will never change, they
try to set me up for my
identity.

Beverly A. Foster
Pitcairn, PA

Mirror Image of Reflections

I stopped today and looked at myself in the mirror.
Looking back at me was an image of a person I have not seen in a long time.
I seen me.
I did not see a title or a version of myself.
I seen the same child I was years ago when I was known only as my name.
I wasn't a mother looking back at me, I wasn't a grandmother, a daughter or broken by any of life's pain.
I was not my mistakes, shortcomings, successes or failures.
I was only me.
I stared at myself feeling stripped down to the bare necessities of my own reflection.
I felt my mind being still.
It is not my place to reflect someone else's pain into my own image when I have a life left to live and they have room left to heal.
In that moment I forgave myself for anything I had done wrong in my life.
I forgave those around me for they are still seeking God's plan.
I felt the presence of God and purity I had been born with.
When I finally turned away from the mirror I knew I was becoming a better version of me.
I like who I am becoming because I remembered how to believe.

Shana L. Boulton
Burlington, IA

Ready? Watching? Waiting?

Are you ready? Are you watching?
Are you waiting?
Alas! I look; I cannot see.

I search all around but
have not found
the wonderful gift of God
that will set me free,
"A Big Star" in the sky.

Did you see it? The star
where the Baby Jesus was born.
"The Jesus" who was to die for our sins,
buried and risen again in three days.

If I believe in His love, Oh! Hey!
I feel His love; Hallelujah!
Oh! If I had wings as a dove,
I'd fly away; "Rapture Hallelujah!"
Oh! Yes, I am ready, watching and waiting.
Rejoice evermore. I Thess. 5:16

Alma Ann Williams
Vardaman, MS

Oh! to rejoice (I Thess. 5:16) I have almost reached the goal line: daughter, wife, mother, grandmother (nani), great-grandmother. God has been so good. I have two grandsons who went ahead of me—an eighteen-year-old with liver cancer and forty-three-year-old bone surgeon. Life can get like an earthquake. God promised to never leave or forsake us. The separation will not be for long. He gave us two little baby boys this October and December. He replaced our loss. I Thess. 5:16 Rejoice evermore!

Jesus Changes Anger into Love

So you have been hurt,
You have had a hard life!
Jesus sees your hurt,
Jesus is hurting right along with you!
So you want to hurt, fight, destroy,
You want to cheat, steal, shout!
Jesus understands your pain,
Even though it seems no one does!
So you think it's not fair,
You think no one cares,
But it's not true,
Jesus cares so much about you!
So you wonder where was Jesus,
Why didn't he stop all this hurt?
But Jesus did put a stop to the hurt
By dying on the cross for everyone's sins,
So they could live in Heaven forever
Where there will never be pain again!
Jesus is waiting for you,
He wants so badly to help you!
Jesus is willing to forgive you!
Jesus can change anger into love!

Angela Christine Michael
Mesa, AZ

Winter's Worries

In comes the cold, some zero below
Then the depression and loneliness grow.
Snow covers the ground as the north wind blows,
And sniffles start with the running of one's nose.
Darkness comes early and the eyes get blurry.
Frozen tears run down the cheek
as life now seems so bleak.
As sadness turns to madness and craziness grows
So does despair as everyone knows.
Feeling sad isn't so bad
As time marches on you'll soon be glad.
As the weather gets warm you will become reborn
And soon you will sing...
Thank God it's spring!

Robert John Vogt
Schenectady, NY

A Heart of Gratitude

I have a heart of gratitude
For all You've given me
I daily reap Your blessings
And I am thankful as can be.

I thank You for the breath of life
For health and strength each day
I am thankful for the food and clothes
You have seen fit to send my way.

I thank You for the sun and rain
For flowers all in bloom
You fill my life with beauty,
There's no place at all for gloom.

Your presence is like sunshine
That lifts my spirits high
You teach me ways to serve You
All I have to do is try.

In the world in which I live
My heart responds with gratitude
As my life to You I give.

Alma M. Gaines
New Rochelle, NY

To Joey

With a smile and a grin
That's how it will be
When I think of
Joey and what he
Meant to me
Always there to
Help with a hand
Stretched out
Never complaining
Never a pout
Today I say farewell
To a good and kind soul
Here's to you, Joey
Let your story be told

Gail M. Wolf
River Grove, IL

Society

Sleepless nights have me
tossing and turning
midnight darkness plays
tricks on the mind
waking up filling drained
and emotionally empty
void, mentally playing tricks on myself
walking into the sunshine
with the evil looks
deadly stares
no wonder we are
the way we are
living in a world of prejudices
looks are everything
if you don't look normal
then there must be
something wrong with you
the mental cycle repeats
continuously without mercy

Jamie Fernandez
Victorville, CA

Dear Uncle Raymond Beckett

Although WWI took you from our
family in 1918, please know you
are not forgotten.

My mother had so many wonderful
memories of you. I wish I could
have known you.

On her death bed mother said,
"Raymond is here with us," and
I believe that you *were* here.

Thank you, God, for sending
Raymond to visit with us.
It was an experience I will
treasure always.

Love,
Gay

Florace G. Hensley
Titusville, FL

*Military records for Raymond Ray Beckett, medic, who was killed in France in 1918.
Enon, WV cemetery*

Winter Got Me

I am dancing March is here
Good news, calendar says spring is near
Good-bye, winter, it's time to think green
With colorful flowers mixed in between
Daffodils, crocus, snowdrops, hyacinths, tulips
Beautiful colors I want to see, happy I will be
My closet will have coats, hats, scarves, and gloves
Gone fierce winds, snow, ice, and bitter cold
My body says I am way too old
A bit of snow almost every day I see
My car an igloo waving to me
Walking carefully I slip and slide
My hands, feet, and nose they freeze
I want to be under the covers on my bed
Farewell to damp, dreary, snow, windy days
I want to sit wearing a sweater, warm sun on my face
I am hopeful, my calendar says spring is near
Shades of green, colors bright, warm sun I invite
But for now I will rush about
Or an iceberg I shall become

Anita L. Rogers
Royersford, PA

At Last

By my heart betrayed
My memories fade
As time grows short
And Death I court.
A sky crystal blue
Speaks of God's love true
Trees with roots deep
Whisper of eternal sleep
So under a bed grass green
Let me lay serene
No more worries; fewer cares
In a world that ne'er shares
When my breath at last does cease
Lord grant that I find peace.

Billy Joe McKee
Mint Hill, NC

Shambles

I am told our once beautiful home
   is now in shambles
   and I breathe a care, for it is there
   we left our hearts.
I am told the Persian carpet
   is now threadbare and soiled.
The golden oak cabinets
   are pitted with paint.
That grand fireplace
   that warmed many a gathering
   is dark and cold,
   choked to death with soot and web.
I am told those walls that absorbed
   love and laughter
   now echo quarrel and hate.
The silk curtains have been shredded by cats
   the basement infected by rats
   the attic spooked with bats.
I wonder if the scent of my wife's clothing
   still lingers in the closet?
I am told our once beautiful home
   is now in shambles.
With one last look I breathe a sigh,
   wave goodbye,
   and drive away.

Richard Raunio
Crystal, MN

Endurance

Nights are lites with star blemishes
around the mellow mist on the grass
of green shadow, when fade drops of
rain that diminishes. The means
of earthly shapes that dices of feeling
and healing, Cloves has a mission of
life, "to surrender true endurth"
memorizing its truth
Everlasting force of dense flubber
that changes in a twinkle of an eye
"True feeling" a habit of heart stabbing
Love within a everlasting force, so that
without the beat of the heart there is no
humming to be done
The truth is no more to see or to be heard
The force that we share can render for
Infinity "Life"

Patricia Ann Allen
Baltimore, MD

Grandchildren

My granddaughter, my world, little miss Mila June
The light of my life so sweet and innocent
She is now three but still a baby in my eyes
She will always be a baby to me
Always a joy to be with. So sweet and innocent
She calls me Grandma and I light up with a big smile
I never thought I would be a grandma but here I am killing it
Makes me so happy I would do anything for her
Little miss Mila June!

Victoria Drost
West Springfield, MA

If

If old I am as wine esteemed I'll treat
If old I am as wine I must be sweet
If love I have will share with those elite
If love I have will share with all I meet
If rich I am shall be a one discreet
If rich I am shall be a humble feat
If health I have a world above I'll greet
If health I have a world shines most complete
If skilled I am to share this go's so neat
If skilled I am to share just can't be beat
If luck I have as fortune's 'neath my feet
If luck I have as fortunes flow I'll eat

Glenn Howard Voirol
Fort Wayne, IN

Dear Brother

As you walk over the hill
Into the sunset land
I'll remember you
In all our favorite places
I'll see you in the spring
When the earth is fresh and green
I'll see your face in the rainbow
After the summer storms
I will remember you in autumn
Through the golden days of harvest
and through the winter
When the snowflakes fall
I'll hear your voice in the wind
I will remember you
Now and forever
'Til we meet again
My brother, my friend

Evelyn Stonesifer
Lecanto, FL

He's Always There

He's always there when you're having difficulties in life.
He's always there and comes thru.
He's always there when others forsake you.
He's always there and will never leave nor forsake you.
He's always there wherever you go in life.
He's always there when you walk alone.
He's always there because you're special.
He's always there moments matter appear dark.
He's always there, call upon Him and He will answer.

Addy Cox
Newark, NJ

Life

Life is like a pond
Deep sometimes murky and dark
It swirls and swirls
When you fall inside

It goes on and on
Takes you along
As your destiny calls

It's your fate
Only God knows about

Mitra Pourmehr
San Rafael, CA

A Boy Needs a Grandma

A boy should have a grandma
To tuck him into bed,
To read him favorite stories
And pat him on the head.
A boy deserves a grandma
When mother's not around,
To spoil him just a little
And bounce him up and down.
A wee boy needs a grandma
To bake him apple pie,
To share with him some laughter
And sing him lullabies.
A fellow wants a grandma
To read him nursery rhymes,
To place him on her lap
And rock and talk about old times.
A boy cries for a grandma
To chase away his fears,
To scare that bad, old bogeyman
And dry up all his tears.
A boy just loves a grandma
Who tells him what to do,
And lets him know she really cares,
I think that grandma's you!

Rebecca J. Bebout
Morgantown, WV

This is a poem for grandmothers everywhere even though I wrote it years ago for my son, Randy, to give to his grandmother, Anita M. Mull, as a Christmas present. I am seventy-eight years old, and Randy is now forty-nine. I live in Morgantown, WV.

My Mom

In the year 1905 from a foreign land she came
Couldn't speak any English and she just turned 16
Settled here in this land she called the greatest country
Doing housework for the rich and working in a jelly factory
My sweet mom
Time moved on and soon she married
Through the depression years she struggled
Raising 8 young ones she carried
Always giving the most to the ones she loved so much
She was dear, always near, never out of touch
My sweet mom
Never losing ground in the battle of survival
She was warm, she was strong and never tiring
Her hair that once was golden brown
Too soon has turned to white
We laid her to rest in the land she loved so much
And the loss was deeply felt by all who were in touch
A tender heart of love and very dear was she
And I thank God 'cause He gave her to me.

Helen Lovett
Plumsteadville, PA

I am ninety-two years of age. This poem is the result of my mom coming over to the US at the age of sixteen. I've written a lot of poetry over the years. My mom had eight kids; I am the last one.

Footsteps Fading

I knew you for a time—where did you go?
You left my world like a distant cloud, a finished dream,
a burst bubble. *Pop*, you went away and left with disarray.
I knew you for a time—you became my friend,
someone I latched on to for a circle of dance.
I took the chance to know you—where did you go!
I felt your footsteps fading as you silently walked away.
You left me there, alone, over and over,
each one of you in your own time and space.
Can't erase those times spent.
Here I exist in a new time cycle—I don't like "them";
they cause too much mayhem,
trouble to endure the immature.
The ghosts of the past to endure...footsteps fading
I still see your faces in all the pleasant places.
Did I expect you to be there forever...
never to sever our connection?
Correction: I will never forget your fading footsteps.
You will be with me in memory, always...
forever glad I took the chance.

Nancy L. Cox
Denver, CO

Hymn for America

Looking down upon America from a mountain peak so high
Stood a young, impassioned patriot,
Noting beauty far and wide.
She saw "purple mountain majesties"
And great "amber waves of grain,"
And the promise of America in the nobleness of man.

She prayed for fallen heroes who built our nation fair,
Who had "more than self their country loved"
And sustained it with their prayers.
And she prayed for God's great mercies,
For His grace upon our land,
Wisdom for our leaders, and the brotherhood of man.

Whether native son or immigrant, former king or slave,
May the human rights we stand upon
And our freedoms never fade.
When we stand upon our mountaintops
Or gaze up from valleys deep,
May we then recall that through it all
We have promises to keep!

Thus may it ever be, "from sea to shining sea,"
God bless America, our home!

Margaret Rose Green
Nokomis, FL

This poem was written to represent a retelling of the events leading Kathryn Lee Bates to write the words later used as lyrics to "America the Beautiful." It is also a reminder of our responsibilities as Americans.

A Leopard

Throughout the centuries and now again in ours
Repeats the cadenced sound of marching feet
To meet the madness with its pounding beat,
Drum, drum, drumming forth the dreaded hours.
Stealthily, man crouches like a leopard,
Straining against the leash to rip apart
Those finely linens, enwrapping smothered
Freedom's wounds and tear up a nations heart.

While the molten-madness roils and rumbles.
The marching gains in pace, the knelling swells:
Leopards leap from out their hidden jungles
With appetites the clenching claw compels.
So, the wars are waged, right, left, left and right
While crickets, without care sing through the night.

Carmen Ruestow
Boulder, CO

An Aubade for a Daughter's Loss

What sadness does the dawn bring
Another death for the new day
So broken in mourning for the loss
My mother passed at the breaking of dawn
She had such a hard life
Survived on her own
Never sacrificed her beliefs to appease others
Brave for us kids
I still hear her soft voice calling me,
I try to answer
And hope she can hear me
We loved her
Now she is gone
At the breaking of Dawn

Marcy Lynette Bowser
Newark, OH

Uplifting True Story

A friend shared with me a video of a wonderful true story;
Events were really interesting and nothing gory;
Love, selflessness, and friendship throughout prevailed;
There was no need to angrily expel;
There was accidental death and corresponding grief;
Heartbreak and injuries subsided and found relief;
The deep devotion for an animal was what it took,
and the sacrificial love for a friend in pain on the hook;
By beholding we are changed,
by wholesome movies unfeigned;
Society could benefit from human interest stories true;
Uplifting stories dispel bad news blues;
If life imitates art and art is good,
what favorable results might be experienced by friends in neighborhoods.

Bernice Hooks
Chicago, IL

Scripture: Philippians 4:8 "Finally, brethren, whatsoever things are true, whatsoever things are honest, whatsoever things are just, whatsoever things are pure, whatsoever things are lovely, whatsoever things are of good report; if there be any virtue, and if there be any praise, think on these things." The world is in turmoil. Let us pray for our leaders and for ourselves to do the right thing. Righteousness exalts a nation. Jesus is coming again in the clouds with bright power and glory. The dead in Christ will rise first. (See 1 Thessalonians 4:16.)

Faces 'N Facets

Michelle Ginger Imig
A woman of many faces,
Michelle, my belle,
Ginger, happy and spicy,
Imig, her looks, smarts and class.
Fade to the face of the daughter,
So child-like, wants her
mommy and daddy near.
Shift to the face of the mother,
So vulnerable, yet so strong,
There in a pinch, there
in the storm...the mother lode!
Look at the face of the sister,
The advisor, the comforter,
The needy one...the protector.
The face of peaches 'n cream,
The guardian of children,
A friend's friend,
Collector of things—
A counselor and a counsel.
The face of life—lively and fun,
Joyful, yet sad,
Coming together—all in a look,
A look on a face— the faces and
Facets of Mickey
Faces 'n Facets, persons and pieces,
Fractured then mended,
Made whole again—portrait of a face
The face of Michelle.

Mary Dell Cody
Yankton, SD

Michelle Ginger Imig now Mickey Tapken of Austin, TX is my older sister. At my seventy-eight years she brings calm and love at her eighty years when we are together. She is everything described in "Faces 'n Facts" and more.

Clinton's Trojan Horse

Clinton designed a Trojan horse
Just for America, of course!
Unlike those clever Greeks of old
It's his own, whom he has sold
A bill of goods, which is no lie!
Let China in! His strident cry.
Hasn't he given them enough?
Special access and other stuff?
National security has been breached!
Thanks to Lee, that smiling leach!
Was this the price of re~election?
Access to covert connection!
May I suggest, we would be wise
On China to not compromise!
If he thinks they are so great
Perhaps Clinton and Hillary should immigrate!

Mary Elizabeth Santomauro
Stagecoach, NV

A Willing Spirit

Jesus was willing to come down to Earth
To be born in a stable, a lowly birth
He was willing to leave His heavenly home
To live among us and leave His kingly throne

He loved us so much, was willing to die on a cross
To save us from eternal death—oh what a cost!
He was cursed, spit on, treated shamefully
All this he did and did it willingly

He died in our place so we could be
With Him in Heaven and live eternally
He kept all His promises, He rose from the dead
He clothes us in His robe of righteousness instead

He says if we believe in Him
We will be saved
History shows that this is true
God is willing—are you?

Oh, Lord, give us a willing spirit
Make us all clean and new
I am willing
And waiting for you

Linda J. Knudsen
North Mankato, MN

Remember Me

You can shed tears
That I'm gone
Or you can smile
Because I've lived.
Your heart will be empty
Or you can let it be full
Of the love we shared together.
You can remember me
And think that I'm gone
Or cherish my memory
And let it go on.
You can live in sorrow
Of yesterday
Or you could
Just do what
I would want you to do.
Greet tomorrow with hope.
Love and go on.

Sheila Evans
Forest City, NC

Snowy Plunge

The car did swerve, I lost my nerve
And every one of us did feel the skid of wheel
And plunging down into the snow-filled bank
The slippery car sank and stuck were we
For none to see and rescue far
Was just a bar, to our escape and twilight take
The light away and there to stay,
A frozen night became fright.
And snowing more, our tires entrenched;
We were all drenched.
So in the snow knee-high deep, we traveled far.
But too wet were we, and fear of frostbite
Became the night.
Back in the car, we ate a bar
Of stale chocolate and crackers found,
Listening to the sound of our car heater motor.
Ten miles from town, no one around,
Despair set in, and we were thin
On Optimism—and pessimism crept in.
But then we turned around and heard the sound
Of breaks of a truck, what luck!
And pushed were we up the hill, then even still
Down we went, as Heaven sent
An Indian angel our way to let us live another day.

Alison Ann Robinson
West Hills, CA

*This poem was an account of a true story when my family and I were on a day trip
from a sunny day in Albuquerque to a lake nearby. The weather took a turn for the
worse and we found ourselves on a one-lane road climbing a hill. As we went down
the hill, it started snowing and our car got stuck in the snow ten miles from town.
Because I am a very spiritual person and a scientologist, I was able to keep a positive
outlook during this time, and we were saved by some Native Americans in their truck.*

The Crayons

They sleep
Standing tall in their high fortress
Like brave soldiers dressed in full color
Each has an important job to do
It is time, the gates open
Their brilliance brings beauty to so many
The canvas explodes with their valor
Imagination is their armor
beauty their victor
The sun rises in brilliant yellows and oranges
Nature is so regal in her tones of green
Wildlife is illustrated at its best
in soft hues of grays and browns
Never has a sky been so radiant or blue
How hard they work,
each with an important job to do
Weary now, they return to the fortress
The gate closes
They sleep

Lynn G. Armstrong
Hammond, LA

Who Do You Say That I Am?

Some say Jesus was a wise man, but only just a man;
    They say His dying happened apart from any plan;
The Greatest Story Ever Told's too good, can't be true;
    The story of a Savior who died for me and you.

Jesus asked His twelve disciples,
    "Who do men say that I am?"
They said, "Elijah, John the Baptist,
    some other prophet-man."
Then Jesus asked of Peter, "Who do you say that I am?"
    Answered he, "The Christ-Messiah,
        the Son of God and Man!"

Jesus asks of every person, "Who do you say that I am?"
    Salvation's in the answer, the question's in His plan.
You must decide who died there on the Cross of Calvary:
    Your Creator or a liar; indifferent you can't be.

If Jesus was not God, then it means He lived a lie;
    So, eat, drink, and be merry: tomorrow you will die.
But if from the tomb He's risen as He promised He'd do,
    Being who He is He'll make this holy pledge come true:
    If He's your Lord and Savior, you'll live forever, too.

Richard G. Rinker
Columbia City, IN

When We Believe

Believe the Word of God for it is the day your heart begins to live in
resurrection power.
A new life began in my heart as I came into the arms of Jesus Christ.
In every breath I gasped for the presence of His love.
Each day rivers of tears rolled down my cheeks as I cried to Jesus my
life story.
Captured through His Love my heart began to live again.
A new identity has risen within me.
Hallelujah! I am not alone for my life belongs to almighty God!
The spirit of the Lord leads me to witness to all nations of people about
the greatest love story ever!
I tell you whosoever is born of God overcomes the world!
I am a world overcomer for I am in Christ and my glory is assured in Him
and my victory!
Faith in God will teach you that nothing else matters but the victory we
have in Christ!
God's Love is everlasting—whose report will you believe?
Every day is a new song in my heart and a new walk.
In my elder years I fall to my knees like a child under the care of my Father.
I am resurrected by your divine presence each moment we share
intimately with a surrendered heart.
I am set free forever in my heart, mind, and soul for a new captain showed
up the moment I believed!

Ipolita Sanchez
Brooklyn, NY

Reflection

I am homo sapiens (at least I think I am). I am God
Almighty, Creator of the entire world
(If I remember it, obviously). I, homo sapiens
Would like to ask you a couple of questions.
You created so many wonderful things, like universe,
Planets, stars. You created all seen and unseen.
You live in every flower, every leaf, and every drop of dew.
Everywhere is You, Your life-giving power.
You created a small blue planet designed as Eden to place
Your most mystical creation—human beings—for them
To live in love, joy and comfort. What was Your goal
In creating this miracle? You spent billions of years to create
Humanity—this unique "substance" you could be proud of.
You endowed human beings with soul and body, mind
And consciousness, imagination and intellect. You even
Suggested an idea of religion to temper their passions.
Are You happy with the outcome? Do humans glorify you
For their unique abilities and the Eden you created for them so
Generously? What inspires humans with wondrous
Persistence—killing, fighting, stealing, hating, destroying
Nature, creating chaos and turmoil all over this long-suffering
Earth... Is your optimism fading like snow and ice on the
Planet? You seem plunged into deep pessimism watching the
Trend mankind is evolving gradually. I, a phenomenal
Creation of yours, would like to give you some advice.
Don't be upset. Take a philosophical point of view on your
Masterpiece (some say it helps).

Elvira Butynskaya
San Francisco, CA

*I am on the verge of my nineties and I am deeply distressed watching the trend we, as
humanity, are evolving. By composing this opus I made an attempt to ponder over the
most important challenge the modern world is confronted with. I tried to analyze the
subject choosing a non-traditional approach mixing deep reflection and irony.*

Hear Us Pray

The shape is irregular.
It needs to be hoed daily. The undergrowth trimmed.
The sun droops and lolls. The moon slips away.
Stars no longer twinkle.
Clouds no longer tinkle.
And God no longer hears.

Let us see.
Let us pray.
More. Not less.
For sanity.
For peace.
For grace.

Helena M. Langley
Granite City, IL

I hope my work speaks to you in a special way. You can read it literally or metaphorically. Life isn't always black and white. Sometimes it's grey. I am an author and artist residing in Granite City, IL.

Springtime

O Springtime, lovely springtime
From the blossoms when it's May
The breeze blows soft and gentle
Perfume of the springtime flowers
Birds and butterflies, I see you
reaching for the sky
I hear the songbirds singing
May shall make the world anew
Celebrate the lovely springtime

Mary King
Denver, CO

This poem is dedicated to my grandson Ryan Michael. As an adult, Ryan was a very helpful person, always helping others. One day he was hurt on his job, had to have surgery which led to a brain injury. After that, he was unable to speak or walk. He fought hard for two years, working with rehabilitation and therapy. Nothing seemed to be helping. On January 20, 2025 the fight was finally over. He went on his journey and crossed over into the afterlife. He loved flowers so this poem was written for him.

The Mourning After

No one tells you about the aftermath
The sleepless nights
The waking in sorrow
Every morning
Night after night
Crying yourself to sleep
The sudden recall
And the flooding of tears
The feeling of the loved one's presence
And quick reminder they're gone
The broken hearts
The loss for you, your children
The loss of time
The loss of hearing a particular laugh
The sharing with a friend
The knowing voice and understanding between souls
That can never be replicated with anyone
Ever again
No one tells you about the mourning after.

Rhonda C. Villanova
Ellington, CT

Rhonda Villanova is a wife and mother of three adult sons. She lives in a small town in Connecticut where she works as a bookkeeper for her local library. She studies health related topics, designs costumes, and creates exhibits as time allows. She also volunteers for multiple organizations and town committees, one of which plans the annual Memorial Day ceremonies and parades, among other things.

Deceitful Lies

Deceitful lies
in a shadow hold with
a mask is worn behind
carrying in an unveiled portray
heavyweight
on the burden
consume to the
spirit soul
shattered hope falls
into pieces by a betrayal of
stabbing knife causing
bleeding to the heart
on an eerie night
echo of resonant sorrow
pain bringing a cast of
teardrop leading to the
grief of flow
a scar of reminder remains
leaving with haunting
memory through an
everlasting
reflecting
of inner
voice display

Hanh N. Chau
San Jose, CA

Painted Pony

Today I am a painted pony and rider, too
Strong thighs and sturdy ribs make us one
My hoofs are thunder
Lightning my streaking mane
Prairie grass furrows as I pass
Crickets and crows scatter and screech
"Who could that be?"
The earth leaps and hurls beneath my rolling hoofs
Nostrils widen as I take on the wind
Toward the mountain I bound
To a place I've never been

Jan Cosmos
Sturgeon Bay, WI

I've been an educator all my life. It's never been a job, only a lifestyle of venturing to new places. Sharing a bit of wisdom that I learned along the way is this: when you're lost, find a horse!

The Gift

Climbing, gravel sliding,
anticipating a turn in the wind.
Distant dreams continue to burn
as the sun fades into the luxuriant land.

I pause and reflect on the surfacing stars.
Shall I remember this journey
with the release of balloons signifying freedom?

Oh, questions, questions of fate still endure
that shadow my distant drum.
Do these quests ever display their cards?

Newly-fallen snow began to cradle my eyelashes
with whispers blowing into the air. Oh, quick
changes and timing. I contemplate again.

My journey began with a triumphant band,
never believing the challenges for the dreamer.
As the snow flurries drape my face,
a record of truths is realized.

Janet Margaret Grabarits-Sforza
Northampton, PA

LA Strong Heroes

The fires came city to city, house to house.
Bells rang the firemen grabbed their gear
and got into the big red fire trucks.
Sirens going off so loud as they drove through
the crowded streets of fleeing residents to the
fire scene. They ran toward
the burning buildings trying to put the fires out,
but flames kept rising. Darkness came
and they tirelessly worked around the clock.
But every block is in flames. Skies are all lit up.
They selflessly devoted their lives to saving others.
They kept going and never gave up.
Other firemen came from near and far to help
put out the wildfires that kept rising.
The brave and fearless firefighters, hungry and tired,
still putting out fires and running into burning homes,
coming back out, rescuing people,
and carrying out animals.
The lives they saved—they are selfless heroes.
Even in the darkness of flames we can rise again
and rebuild again in unity and love.

Margo Pennella
Jackson, NJ

I wrote this poem in honor of all the firemen, first responders, medical professionals, and others. They showed tremendous courage and sacrifice as they battled this tragic disaster that affected so many lives. We pray for all who lost family members and pets and their homes and businesses and schools. Together we can help one another rebuild our communities so our families can come together again.

Believe in Yourself

Believe in yourself; set yourself free
See the amazing person you can be
Face all your challenges head on
Don't doubt yourself; let all fears be gone

You are stronger than you even know
Ride the rolling waves, the highs and lows
Take control of everything you know
Let those creative juices flow

Listen to your heart, feel the reggae beat
Overcome all the obstacles you meet
Let your spirit soar even higher
Your unstoppable, spirit's on fire

Let go of the past; it is no more
Live in the present; open the door
Become the best person you can be
Believe in the future; set yourself free

Believe in the future; set yourself free
Believe in the future; set yourself free
Believe in the future; set yourself free
Believe in the future; set yourself free

Leslie Powell
Los Angeles, CA

I am a poet and peace activist turned recent song writer. I write about peace, love and unity, including self-love. My poem encourages people to "Believe in Yourself" and be the best person you can be. It is part of my reggae album, in process. I am listed in Matques Who's Who in America and Who's Who in American Women. I received 2018 Sebert Nelsen Marquis Lifetime Achievement Award, and was selected for their Who's Who in the World. Please find some of my songs on You Tube.

Somewhere

We all live somewhere.
Somewhere usually has a physical address.
Sometimes somewhere is our only ID.
Defining us in some way,
Bringing hints of status and taste
In a database of details.
But somewhere has its limits.
Somewhere, after all, is not everywhere
And it is certainly far from nowhere.
I live in Anacortes,
Washington,
But often spend time at my other address:
At the intersection of History and Imagination
Where truth is found.

Robert Skeele
Anacortes, WA

Alzheimer's

I would have you remember, my darling
As darkness approaches and memory dims
That image of hope caught up in the words
Of Albert Camus, that you so loved and taught
Those bright young minds that defined your life

"Great ideas sometimes slip into the world
as gently as doves"

That beyond the tumult and the striving
Of lives and nations and fading thoughts
There lies, enshrined in light eternal,
an all transforming love

As you struggle in that battle of polar opposites:
Clarity and confusion
Cognition and incoherence
Intellect and indifference

Remember my precious one
That you are never alone
But borne up by the soft flutter of wings
In beauty, power, and supernal love

William Stansmore
Loveland, CO

*This poem is dedicated to my beloved wife, Linda, who died from this terrible disease.
She loved this precious earth of ours so much, she formed the environmental studies
program at Columbia University to help preserve its beauty. It's a terrible thing to
watch a brilliant mind slowly fade away.*

Vanish

When the words vanish
May thoughts and memories
Remain to bring comfort
For time spent within the years
Vanished from here and now
Words may not be heard
Memories are what remain
Keeping the vanished near
Until they can be heard
Once again
Within the wind may
A smile reach those still here
From a rainbow to a ray of light
May the vanished be seen
With a butterfly seen within the daylight
May the vanished be felt
To bring a smile and hope
With those who are still here
The vanished shall be near
If only for a moment
The vanished are here
With you

Michael L. South
Kremmling, CO

Together Alone Again

Look at all the heads bent down.
Some have a smile. Some have a frown.
Just wanted to see some friends,
But everyone is busy with texts and sends.

Fingers flying at an amazing speed,
But a touch or a swipe is all I need.
Here I am! Just give me a grin.
Some human attention I just can't win.

Eyes that never ever look up.
Hands too busy to raise a cup.
Oh excuse me, I have to go.
Someone is calling that I don't know.

I've tried to find myself a place,
But I get lost between edit and space.
Together alone again and so sad.
If I didn't love you, I'd be texting mad!

Tina K. Stoneking-Trujillo
Taos, NM

MAGA

I felt the darkness lifting
When Trump got voted in
The evil has been broken
Exposing those in sin.

The world is turning to Jesus
Back to what is pure and clean
Now our hope has been renewed
Man helping man is being seen.

Trump is trying to stop the wars
We pray and believe peace will come
Help them to see and understand
To walk in love is the victory won.

Only God can change a heart
The changes come from within
President Trump has a strong anointing
But God, Makes America Great Again

Shalom Christina Zoë
Roswell, NM

Love Is Timeless

When I first met you,
Time stood still.
Something had changed,
The sun rose over the hill.

Then the sun shone bright.
Midday came.
Our love prospered,
Nothing was ever the same.

Time has passed,
Night is near.
Yet love is timeless,
You are ever my dear.

Kenneth D. Swan
Marion, IN

In a world too often characterized by hatred and destruction, it is good to remember that love endures and is timeless. Love is of God. Much depends on our perspective and how we view others and the world: Love shapes what we see, what attitude we have, and how we react.

Anything

Anything, anything I say
That's certainly a surprise
More than I can surmise
Should I consider lots?
There could be many plots
Mind boggling to myself
Could it be riches or love?
Perhaps from Heaven above!
Maybe, anything is always!
Always I will remember you!
Your kindness, faithfulness, and love
All the wonderful things you do
What is life without you?
You are always the same
With you there is no blame
Dear God...
You I will proclaim!
Always more than anything!

Bonnie Jean Manning
Johnson City, TN

Estranged

Here am I, Little Bird, seeking crumbs.
One will sustain me, for a while.
I watch. I pray.
I knock, I hunt, I seek and scratch.
Will I enjoy a banquet one day?

I felt you visit today.
Chimes gifted from you quivered outside my door.
I hope you are happy, well, at peace with life.
Your 'Little Bear' abides with me.
Sometimes a wistful smile, sometimes mournful eyes,
he'll whisper encouragement:
"He's working things out."

He is all of you that I can hold,
your absence an albatross of sorrow.
His softness, a brush of your hair,
memory of heart stories shared.
I am tormented by the question,
"Will we share any tomorrows?"

I couldn't ask that we be as before.
The distance, the time, the silence,
all thieves of your presence.
Still, here am I, hungry, sad, enduring in my steadfast vigil.
Here am I.

Carolyn M. Massey
DeKalb, IL

Ready to Sleep

When the world is asleep, only me awake,
there is a voice deep within me late into the night.
It is then I think clearly, it is then I write.
God's humble gift are the words I create.

Life we proclaim is a continuing journey,
leery curiosity gently, silently guiding me
down a meandering river, up a snow-covered peak.
Paths that were chosen, answers I seek.

Darkness surrounds me, dawn drawing near,
My eyes grow weary; I close them in prayer.
Asking forgiveness and mercy, I know He will hear.
His glory consumes me, year after year.

Tonight I will dream softly, my task is complete.
Tomorrow here shortly... I'm ready to sleep.

Renette JoAn Colwell
Prescott, AZ

I Cry for You

America, you've turned your face from God's grace.
You've let greed and idolatry take his place.
Self-centeredness and apathy have found a strong hold.
Our way of life, we have sold.
The family unit that once was strong
now hardly exists—that's wrong!
If parents aren't teaching their children the right song,
how can they know right from wrong?
The moral fiber of this country is being torn
with drugs, violence, child abuse, and porn.
God once blessed this great land,
but time runs out as an hourglass' sand.
I cry every night for this once great land
and ask God to bless us again with His loving hand.

Sherry Cappallo
Corsicana, TX

Time

Time
goes on
and on
an on
and on
an on
and on
an on
and then
Stops

Ethelyn June Barnes
Kansas City, MO

Queries for the New Year

What beloved family members will leave us?
Who will star in this year's blockbuster movie?
What will the top news story of the year be?
What scientific breakthrough will astonish us all?
Who will appear on the political scene to mystify us?
What will be the word of the year?
Who will be the next internet feline star?
What will the scandal of the year be?
What will happen that will change your life?
Truly, only the next twelve months know the truth.

Joelle Margarete
Northern California

The Rise and Fall of Heroes

Being pushed into service to protect
and defend another country's nation
that had asked for America's help
to win back its freedom once again
from the communist rule in southeast
Asia! That had taken its toll upon this
unprepared land as has also been done to ours.
Young heros' lives as they knew it were
gone into the swamps and jungles of Vietnam.
Suddenly they were placed in where...
death and loss of friends was an everyday
event, also thinking of one's family and friends.
As death surrounds these young heroes,
as they all hope they'll make it back home alive.
This experience had changed all their lives.
Some could no longer face the men they
had become—so they changed themselves
instead with tattoos and piercings until
other people couldn't recognize him.
Until one day, years later cancer became
his next door neighbor and wouldn't leave him
alone. Until this past December he suddenly died.

Poet A. Crickett
Clintonville, WI

All Colors Matter

All of us are in a race.
All of us have roots to chase.
Follow your roots, see where they go.
They may lead to something you didn't know.

Like maybe some distant cousin
With a different color of skin.
With this fact pounding in your mind,
Could this change your thinking of mankind?

You do know we have interchangeable parts?
This includes our blood and our hearts.
A human's skin sure creates a lot of chatter.
But the fact is all colors matter.

What does the color of a person's skin
Have to do with what's within?
Use their eyes to look through.
You may see a world you never knew.

Our goal in life should be to thrive
And to help all of mankind to survive.
The truth that we all must face
Is all of mankind's colors are in the *human race*.

Steven M. Trobridge
Portland, IN

On Your Special Day Jacob and Sarah

8-3-24
On this your wedding day
We wish you more than we can say
It's the start of your lives together
As husband and wife forever
We pray you have many a day
Where love and laughter come your way
Till death do you part as they say
In seventy years or more for sure
We pray for many youngsters running about
And lots of time to enjoy them
If ever you should doubt
Just pray to God to work it out
Live, love, laugh every day
May God bless you on this day!
Every anniversary we will say
God has blessed you in every way!
No man shall break this bond
I'm happy to say for an eternity
Your love will last forever and a day!
Bless you both on this your wedding day
To have and to hold till the end of time
God bless you!

Debra Jo Rogers
Germantown, OH

I wrote this poem for my friend's son and wife to celebrate their wedding day. It's nice to commemorate their special day! Thanks for making this possible. It's my gift to them to last a lifetime in print and in my heart. These young people went to Africa for their honeymoon to help with buildings by painting and cleaning and teaching life skills to young women—amazing!

Jesus and Jimmy

Your pictures are lined
on my desk at home
You watch as I write
my life in a poem

Jesus keeps me sane
Jimmy keeps me entertained

Songs painfully remembered
come easier in time
I put my pain on paper
and make it rhyme

Jesus keeps me sane
Jimmy keeps me entertained

Happy and sad times
we had them both
Now it's time to move on
for much-needed growth

Jesus keeps me sane
Jimmy keeps me entertained

Elinore J. Krause
Renton, WA

Each night as I go to sleep I say my prayers and thank God for all of the lessons learned in my life and the wonderful music that soothes my soul. I feel so grateful and blessed. (Jimmy Hendrix is the musician.)

Divergent Travails

Old Walter with loud voice decried
Two roads in a wood diverged and I
Took the one less traveled by
And that has made all the difference

But who's to know before betook
Which road is best that leads to brook
For paths don't speak about their look
Their ken revealed to strangers

One took to left a'fourteen breeds
Perchance success but spirit bleeds
To try the often inbred lead
One's nature darkening maybe

Success be-grant a steadfast vow
An ingrained gift a-fixed firm now
False coupling forgiven low
Another path now chosen

Mistakes oft made averred from doom
Self-made choices fill the room
Forgiven oft until the tomb
Beckons till salvation

Douglas Allen Noel
Aiken, SC

The Time That Ran Away

The time we have together
Travels at the speed of light
Each day runs into the next
As we grow closer to the end
So we guard our time together
And keep our love so close
That nothing can separate us
Until death do us part
We are older now
And time goes faster still
But our hearts are ever young
And our love will never part
Time runs faster or so it seems
And our light dims a bit
But love never surrenders
And closer together we become

Lee E. Hedstrom
Oakdale, MN

Daughter

I remember the day you were born, on that September morn
I was so glad about being a dad

A boy I thought you'd be but the Lord threw me for a whirl
And out popped a girl before I could see

Right from the start you stole my heart
I was a father now and had to figure it out somehow

Your little bod was a gift from God
He blessed me with a daughter and the honor of being a father

I loved you more than you ever know as I watched you grow
Learning to walk and learning to talk

We traveled a lot over the years and shared a few tears
If you only knew how proud I am of you

You're all grown with kids of you own
A boy and two girls who mean the world

All I can say is "Wow" I am a grandfather now
We all have so much fun keeping me young

It may not always show
I love you more than you know

Lee Pinder
West Palm Beach, FL

Do You Recall Y2K?

Y2K is an acronym for the twenty-first century,
When all technology would crash and lose memory.
For years, governments and businesses planned
To avert the looming catastrophe at hand.
Spending millions on consulting superpowers
And untold internal resources and man hours.
When the clock strikes midnight,
The Julian calendar might ignite!
Chicken Little screamed, "The markets will fail!"
Brokers and investors drank many cocktails.
New Year's Eve, nineteen ninety-nine,
Enjoy the party before joining the bread line.
On January first we woke in anticipation,
But technology was buzzing with action.
A quarter-century filled with nightmares?
More likely a generation of no one who knows or cares.

Lance S. Loria
Montgomery, TX

I live in sleepy Montgomery, TX, on Lake Conroe. My Bachelor of Science is in accounting, Stetson University, DeLand, FL. I'm currently semi-retired/self-employed management consultant/CPA. I've lived a life filled with professional accomplishments of which I'm proud; however, I'm most proud of my two children. One is a schoolteacher with two sons who are young gentlemen. My other child is a talented musician, song writer, and much more who works within the creative music industry. I'm now in my mid-seventies living life in my lake home where writing is a pleasure and not a pressing deliverable of my professional client work. In addition to poetry, I write short stories and I'm close to completion of my first novel.

Mary Never

I have never thought but I bet Mary never
      knew all the things that her Son Jesus could do.
Like for instance save our souls and heal
      me and you.
He can walk on water and calm the raging seas.
He can fill us with His Holy Spirit when we
      seek Him, yes you and me.
He can make the blind to see and the deaf to hear.
I bet when they saw or heard Jesus speak, their
      hearts were filled with cheer.
He can make the lame to walk and teach the
      mute to talk.
But after everyone had seen Jesus healing the people
      then everyone started to talk.
Some talked out of love and they needed healing, too.
But some talked out of confusion and they weren't sure
      what to do.
But Jesus is the Ruler of our hearts and this land.
For Jesus is the Alpha and Omega for He is the
      great I Am.
Jesus has control of my heart to this very day.
He helps me in my life in all sorts of ways.
So you see when Mary gave birth, Jesus was alive
      in those days.
Now in 2025 Jesus is still alive and doing miracles every day.
I thank You Jesus for Your healing and all that You do.
Thank You that You're in my life and I will always love and
      exalt You, too.

Marsha Melton
Marshville, NC

A Daughter of God

A daughter of God is who you are
God's creation just like the stars
He made you special that I know
And loves you so much thru your beauty it shows

So may God bless you in abundance every day
In all you do, in every way
There is just this one thing
I want to give you this ring

It's just a ring between spiritual friends
And the diamonds will shine to the end
You've earned it by being my most special friend
And it will remind you of now and remind you of then

You are the most beautiful woman I've ever seen
And the ring will remind you of just what I mean
I'll never be able to express the love that I feel
So in front of you now as I kneel

Will this daughter of God be mine
And allow me to love her throughout time
Will she allow me to be the luckiest man
And put this ring on her hand

A beautiful daughter of God above
A woman whom I truly love
I hope that you will be mine
For as long as the stars and diamonds shine

Michael Warren Hartl
Manheim, PA

Memory

Nothing but a memory
Is all that's left.
My heart it just sits
Upon this empty shelf.

It was all just a dream
For me to reminisce—
An illusion of a love
That can only be a wish.

It's time to move on so
Leave the past behind.
'Twas a lesson learned
From a love so unkind.

Now it's time to love
And love the self alone.
None can turn back time
For this love is my own.

The memory lives on;
All the good shall remain.
The bad will balance out;
Along with it is the pain.

I've cried out the hurt,
Learning to live day to day,
Being grateful for it all
And finding peace as I pray.
It is now just a memory of yesterday...

Carolyn Hines
Rosemead, CA

Surface Ripples

Ker plunk! The rock sunk.
Seven feet of clear water teetering it down
As echoing circles ran back to the riverbank.
Ker plunk! Another rock sunk.
A meadowlark applauded in sweet lullaby.
The lazy sun fell down from the sky.
Only a busy dragonfly noted time slip by.
Ker plunk! Another rock sunk.
My thoughts fell deeper than the surface below,
An antipode away, a much darker same day.
Cold and desolate, devastation of unjust death.
A never-ending war, a country's last breath.
Hungry children left clinging to lifeless chest.
No hope left. Oh God, can this be...true?
A horn blast behind my back. I jump to see
A carload of people waving at me.
"We will save you a spot!" a neighbor yelled
As they headed to the park outside of town
For the weekly gathering of our community.
Music from guitars, drums, and all the brass,
Beach blankets, burgers, soda, and ice cream,
A place to share what you had, help whom you could,
All for the greater good. We were living the dream.
Ker plunk! I was long gone before it sunk.

Sara Laureen Bursch
Minnesota

Enjoying Language through Poetry

can you enjoy pure language
the sheer joy of communication
the listening, speaking, reading, and writing
without the constraints of conventions

no regard for correctness
in grammar or formal writing
in format or sentence structure
nor in capitals or punctuation

it is in poetry, language at its best
with the pure sound of pronunciation
the rhythm and recognition of the words
and the scribbling on a page

whether a snapshot as a moment in time
put together with feeling, description, an event
a character, emotion, or anything you express
enjoy the breath of language in a piece of poetry

Joyce Bogdan
West Hartford, CT

Mystery Lake

There is a lake named Mystery which isn't far away;
Wildlife congregate there for thirst and for play.
Eagles exert rule over this varied domain
By soaring and diving to exercise refrain.
Yawning alligators sleep on the sandy shore;
Sleeping the best are the ones who snore.
In argument, two large deer with clashing horns
Will certainly leave one family to mourn.
In proud exclaim, seven turkeys in concert bloom,
With audio mistaken, all seven are out of tune.
A wolf lies exhausted in an earned rest to be,
Safe from the pack in his run to be free.
Wily Bobcats are runners challenging each other,
The loser discernible, listen to the purring mutter.
Coyotes love to play a game called water tennis;
They use their long tails for the racquet menace.

Garry O. Hanson
Florence, KY

*I am a semi-retired consulting engineer who enjoys the challenge of writing poetry as
a pastime. I own a mostly wooded acreage in an area which is quite remote and fifty
miles from where I live. When I saw on the property map that a pond once existed on
this property, I was inspired by a friend to write this humorous fictional portrayal of
what animal life must have been like at that time.*

The Desert Calls

I do not belong in the Midwest
My heart my soul are in Arizona
Whenever I hear a coyote howl
The desert calls out to me

Once in awhile I catch an aroma
That reminds me of mesquite and sage
There is a tree here with thorns
Which reminds me of the cactus

My memory takes me back
When the sun reminds me of hot desert air
Tree shadows dance in the moonlight
Like elk spooked by a wolf

Water runs from my eyes
Swift as a flashflood in a monsoon
When my soul cannot hold back the pain
Of not being where I belong

Sharon Eoff
Moscow Mills, MO

I came to the Midwest to help my daughter through her cancer scare and now five years later the Arizona desert is calling me home. If you are a desert rat you know what I am talking about.

Forever Blessed

I can't move
Literally stuck
I can barely see
What's in front of me
So I'm trusting my faith
Will lead me the right way
Time's been hard
But these bills are due
Rent has to be paid
So I still go to work
Put a smile on my face
Do what I have to do
To make it through the day
But inside I'm hurt
Got a lot of pain
So I pray and ask God to take it away
But it's still here
God how much longer must I endure?
'Cause I fell down bad
And I can't get up
God I need your strength to lift me up
'Cause right now I want to give up
God said stand up and have no fear
I've been here, and I'm not going nowhere
At your worst, you still gave your best
With this attitude, you will always be blessed.

Anzel Nichols
Stone Mountain, GA

Dark Passing of Shadowy Nights

Cast the light as a staff
For before them all a serpent crawls
With these harmless doves to speak of
Speaking forth desire as fire
With this darkness before and after the fall
And of us caught up in an end
To meet again and to be meet in him
Let the little ones be encircled by fire
As glory is overshadowed by a word
Still, sweet in sound and a savory incensed smell
Receive this by and by
And do not hide those things from him
In which they could not see
And in that the acts of darkness are spoken in the light
Let your acts of light be spoken in the dark
Come away with me and receive eternity
This end of all, both here and now
With a beginning stand then
Bear the light and pass over its night and strike
Strike down those who would not be heard
A record to remember with words feared and revered
Bring them before the light
To be spoken in this dark passing of shadowy nights

Mark A. Cloutier
Kailua, HI

Poem of Romantic Song Titles

Over the mountains across the sea ... image of a girl
I look at you
What's your name
Oh girl ... Gee whiz
Could it be I'm falling in love ...
Will you love me tomorrow
Betcha by golly wow
What am I living for
Only you
Since I met you, baby
In the still of the night
Oh what a night ... let's get it on
I can't stop loving you
Since I fell for you
You're my everything
I live for your love
Talk to me ...
You make me feel brand new
When I am with you
How sweet it is
Hooked on a feeling
When a man loves a woman
Love and happiness
Let's stay together
I love you for sentimental reasons ...

Arturo Cantú Hernández
San Antonio, TX

Mercy Is Now

Come accept God's mercy
While mercy is still free
Mercy was bought by Jesus
On the cross at Calvary
But if you refuse His mercy
Vultures come feed on the humans
The ones who would not bow
Their knees
Hear their plea for mercy after
They lived life as they pleased
No love for God was in them
No sacrifice of self
Vultures come feed on the humans
For there is no mercy left.

Judith A. Stanley
Henderson, KY

I Be Forgetting

I be forgetting where I put my keys;
Sometimes I have to look for them on my knees.

I be forgetting to pay a bill;
That also includes taking a pill.

I be forgetting if I have to go to the doctor;
I ponder and wonder as I sit in my rocker.

I be forgetting where I put the remote control for the TV;
Because of this, I cannot watch the programs I want to see.

I be forgetting to call family and friends on Sunday;
Sometimes I may not remember to do so until Monday.

I be forgetting to get coffee, sugar, and creamer from the store;
This has happened many times before.

I be forgetting birthdays and my anniversary;
Charge it to my head and not to me.

I be forgetting to do what I say;
Don't take it personal, it just happens that way.

I just be forgetting…

Raymond A. Thomas
Richmond, VA

I Live at St. Luke's

I live at St. Luke's
I have for a while
Once a month
I break down and smile

It's not that it's good
It's not that it's bad
The problem is
I feel very sad

My life is soon over
Whether I want it or not
But, living here is
All that I've got

Every day is the same
Nothing is new
I think of the past
That's all I can do

My life has been wonderful
A big thank you to all,
My husband and children
Who won't let me fall

Kayla Kimball
Blue Earth, MN

Remember

Remember now as time travels
side to side in a
sphere
Today it's not what we
think but imagined
So our minds are narrow
to bend as we sleep
We try to live a lie
that wither vapor
Remember now as it was
for tomorrow may never come
Breathe today but
exhale tomorrow

PJ Olivas
Needville, TX

God's Plan....Not Mine

To have this emptiness filled,
I needed to be healed.
It was possible when I put God in place
Of that deep, dark empty space.
It was located right at my gut level;
No amount of booze could make it full.
By letting God replace that spot,
Peace could be brought.
This spirituality being sought
Gave me hope and less distraught.
I can smile and have a positive personality;
Then, I am healed and calmness comes to reality.
My plans got me nowhere;
Life was full of despair.
My instincts were misdirected;
My priorities were neglected.
God's plan for me was always there;
His world was full of hope and care.
His will was so divine,
God's plan....not mine.

Erik William Dittmar
Katy, TX

A New Perspective

I went to get my hair cut
I met a man while there
A stranger when I walked in
But a story he did share
He didn't have to say a word
It was there upon his hat
His story written in his presence
About the dangers of combat
I paid the lady for his cut
With tears he asked, "Why did you do that?"
I put my hand on his head, looked him in the eye
I said, "Because of all you did for us"
I'm so glad you did not die
He was a US Marine vet
Both of his legs he had lost
Trying to keep us safe and free
For that he paid a huge cost
He said, "Now I can buy a hamburger"
As I helped him out the door
I thanked him for his service
Told him I'd be thankful forevermore
My problems seemed so many
Like there was no hope in sight
But after I met this hero
My problems seemed so light

Heidi Mae Hayes
Elkhart, IN

It's the American Flag

It's the American flag in the U.S. of A
It stands for freedom every single day.
For all those who died so we can be free,
Old Glory flies proud for each one to see.

It's the American flag and in war did prevail
with every endeavor but never did fail.
Every day celebrates freedom for all
seasons of winter, spring, summer, or fall.

It's the American flag and this country we stand
a true dedication for the love of our land.
Every day we give our true appreciation
for those who gave their lives in freeing our nation.

It's the American flag called red, white, and blue
with the good and the bad it always flies true.
The "Star Spangled Banner" are words that we sing;
it is the message of freedom that it always will bring.

Edward Edgar Dupre
Palm Coast, FL

Poetry has always been a language that resonates deeply within me. My poetry is of various themes, including dreams and desires to the spiritual depth of my faith. Words have the power to capture my own life experiences that can connect with others. This is what drives me to write poetry.

Think Positive

Go strong in the day
Let love and hope be your inspiration
To guide you on your way
The time is now, the sun is up
I learned what it meant to feel blessed
And what it meant to feel more positive
So get ready for the future but enjoy the present
If life is anything, it's just this moment

Reflect and don't dwell on the past
Live in the present all you can
Look ahead the future is bright
Take hold of life with both hands

Never lose sight of hopes and dreams
True happiness you will find
What you've been looking for all this time
Just say to yourself, "you can do it, have faith, believe you can"

Don't be hard on yourself
I know what it feels like
So hard, I need a friend to help me get it
To guide me on the right track of life

Have comfort in yourself
Think positive not negative
Hang in there even if it's hard
Trust me I know
Be positive for the rest of your life
Have the experience of a lifetime

Danielle Elizabeth Barry
Myerstown, PA

Nothing Is Forever

When I was younger, I thought things last forever;
Only God and our souls last, as we fully surrender.
We return to dust, and none are promised tomorrow;
I realized those thoughts no longer hold through.

We are all born with a purpose; He wants us to prosper,
If we go through darkness, there is light in prayer.
It is hard to choose the difficult narrow path;
The wider path is easier and discernment so far apart.

Where have all the days, time, and all the chances go?
Where are our loved ones, once so close and true?
The laughter is gone, only precious memories remain.
Can we live without regrets as our eyes grow dim?

Is our life what could have been or of what then?
Are our choices aligned with His Will, or just a dream?
Our chaotic world signals that everyone should repent;
God's unfathomable love and mercy has been sent.

As our remaining days go by like the blink of an eye,
So is His second coming; we know not when, but why.
May we turn to God's commandments, follow his flock.
Nothing is forever; we will hear the loud ticking clock.

Virgilia A. Smith
Marshall, MI

The global news headlines inspired this poem. Look back the past few years. We had wildfires, typhoons, hurricanes, floods, earthquakes, wars and rumors of wars, poverty, violence, unbelief of God's words, disrespect of human life, and abortion. Since the US Supreme Court legalized abortion in 1973, over sixty million preborn have been killed and 1,026,700 last year. God loves us, His children. He is our Savior with authority and power. God's final judgement will come soon enough. May we all wake up from our deep slumber and know that He is our only God. He is in charge and in control.

There Goes the Sun

My wife Lisa and I drove up to see the total solar eclipse of 2024
on April the 8th in Erie, PA
When we started our journey it was a partly cloudy day
People from far and near came and invaded this Lake Erie coastal town
The atmosphere was party filled for what was about to go down
Even NASA showed up to watch the lunar show along the Erie shore
There were booths selling hats, T-shirts, stickers and more
Lisa and her friend Judy and I sat in our lawn chairs in an open field
wearing our special eclipse glasses
We were totally separated from the crowded hysterical masses
As we waited for the moon's orbit to cross the path of the sun
We knew it was going to be a celestial spectacle for everyone
The total solar eclipse was something to witness and behold
There was a dark circle with a bright glowing ring of gold
The temperature dropped and it got real dark
You couldn't hear a bird sing or even a dog bark
It was an awesome experience that we'll never forget
However the five hours it took us to drive home that I regret

Skip Clayton
Coraopolis, PA

Rides

It all started with a tricycle;
Soon it was too small.
Bicycles were next—boys and girls,
Old or new, I liked them all.

Spookie the cow was a good ride.
The grey mule was great; Jim was his name.
The horse was a pretty one;
Both big and powerful, I rode him just the same.

Once on an elephant and a camel;
That elephant was so big.
A hot air balloon came after the animals,
But I would never ride that pig.

Boats, planes, and trains were nice.
Big or little didn't matter; I still had a ball.
Can't forget the cars and trucks;
From things I've ridden the car is best of all.

Beth Wallace
Greenbrier, AR

Penguins and Polar Bears

Where do the penguins and polar bears play...
The ice shelves sadly are melting away.
Where do the deer and the antelope play
Forests gutted, clear-cut and scorched
Hinder shelter, gathering, thriving.
Where do sea turtles, fish and otters play
Whilst dancing menacing in their way
Are floating and sinking plastic bottles.
Where do the children play underneath a
Polluted sky...rain and snow falling upon
Them tainted with microscopic plastic particles.
Species starving for sustenance on the brink
Of extinction, collapsing ecosystems threaten
God's survival blueprint for us all.
Global warming, solar flares, extreme freezing
Spells a clear and present danger to our way of life.
So we the concerned sound the alarm...
The watchdog lighthouse in a looming storm.
Those of us who are aware see the signs,
Ultimately fear the demise of our God-given planet.

Jill J. Shaw
Saint Joseph, MO

Native Americans understand preserving the natural abundant resources of our unique and exquisite planet. Our duty as human beings is to protect wildlife and resources, respecting what God has given us. Wildlife species are under duress, in serious danger of extinction. We must speak for those who cannot speak for themselves. According to Canadian news reports, scientists concur: the reality is global warming. Less concerning to me are electric vehicles, which most Americans cannot afford. My deepest concern is: the longevity of endangered species, drastic environmental climate change which is dire, affecting the survival of all of Earth's inhabitants.

A Wonderful Walk in the Forest

Walking in the forest in Sugarloaf today
It is so beautiful on this peaceful Sunday
The breeze in my hair—golden sun on my face
As I walk my prayers are for God's saving grace

Heavenly blue sky and radiant sun above
This is my church surrounded by His love
Sweet Jesus I praise You and it is You I adore
With You by my side there is nothing I want more

Bluebirds and pine trees are so beautiful to see
My heart is full of gratitude—shine your light on me
I walk with a smile and happily think to myself
Praise You Lord for blessing me with good health

Thank you for making me humble and whole
And by Your grace for saving my precious soul
You have shown me the sacred keys to Heaven
In spite of my many difficult life's lessons

My life would be empty, Lord, without You by my side
Now gone is the loneliness and tears that I have cried
May beauty and love in my heart always abide
Walking in the forest it is so glorious to be alive

Judy Russell
Sugarloaf, CA

Forgive Me

Forgive me, my mind gets foggy,
my heart fills with pain,
the tears fall like a hard rain.

Forgive me, my impatience and
bursts of intolerance, my emotions
are all over the spectrum.

Forgive me, my silence, not
meant to be mean nor rude,
don't want to trigger my
sorrowful mood.

Forgive me, don't judge me.
I just need to be numb now
and then. It helps me to
cope with my grief.

Forgive me, I can't say goodbye
to you—to us. Our sisterly
bond has always been pure and
strong, for which I don't
need forgiveness.

Laura Lyn Regusci-Parrish
Sun Valley, NV

The Fall Moon

Once upon a time
I watched a mid fall full moon
Whilst holding my love's soft hands
The silvery ripples danced on the water
As the waves gently ran their journey to the sea
My heart resonated swiftly
With its irregular beats
Such felicity of the hour
Sealed with a soft tender kiss
To remember for a thousand falls
Love, in its splendored mask
Gently surrounded our bewitched souls
We were just in love
As we lived a dream within an ineffable dream
Time had somehow stopped
And we did not have a single care
We heard each other's hearts' tender beats
Within murmurs on our lips:
"Dearest love: Just come closer—yes, my love"

Quoc Sung Truong Ducam
Santa Clara, CA

Desperation to Inspiration

What can change our feelings
of despair into wanting to
inspire others in our life,
especially after losing a
husband or a wife.

Maybe the best way to end
feelings of despair is by
showing others that we care,
even when the grief is almost
too much to bear.

There will be a time when
despair happens to us all
and we may try to separate
ourselves with a protective wall.

Always feeling pain from
the past or fear of the future
is not any way to live.
It is much better to inspire
others with a heart that only
knows how to love and forgive.

This would be a great gift
for all humankind.
And by doing this, we just
might find the peace of
mind we thought we would
never find.

Cathey Paytas
Scottsdale, AZ

Mindful Experience

There can be so much magic in the mundane,
like the way you feel standing in downpouring rain,
the way water swirls when it goes down the drain,
or how blood is blue when it's still in the vein.

There's beauty in what we allow ourselves to see,
not with our eyes, but with our being.
There are some things we can only feel,
but the things in our hearts feel the most real.

Upbeat music to dance; slow music to think;
hot water to bathe; cold water to drink;
warm smiles and uncontrollable laughter.
A mindful experience is what I am after.

Becca Lynn Grant
Beacon Falls, CT

Untitled

Our journey began on Prairie Avenue,
just little girls, me and you.
Little Kiddles, Cootie and hide-n-seek,
our childhood was not unique.
Our lasting bond is our power,
measured in decades, days, minutes and hours.
My first memories are of you,
and our neighborhood on Prairie Avenue.
Having no way of knowing back then,
I'd come to depend on you again and again.
I've had no friendship longer,
no bond stronger.
Since we were four,
need I say more.

Holly C. Hansen
Spring Hill, FL

Written for my lifelong friend Deb A. Falco. I'm grateful for your friendship, love, and support. I love you always and forever.

Endless Oceans

Oceanic orbs, steadily studying,
Pools, spiralling, enticing.
Erotically, they hold me
Captivating and inspirational.
She holds me in place,
Flesh turned to stone!
A fantasy turned upside-down and,
Yet, my heart thunders in my chest,
My veins running hot.
I have no words, but my own reflection says the story.
Bashful and quiet, I stand,
Staring at endless oceans,
Hand stretching out to caress its waters.
Yet, before my fingers touch
The forbidden rule flashes in my mind;
I retract my hand, although I stare longingly in her eyes.

Ezekiel J. Watkins
Renton, WA

Reaching Out

Lord, we seek to start a new task
Lending our talents for whatever you ask
Seeking new ways to help those in need
Be it a community project or a family to feed

We look forward to what the day brings anew
Please give us the guidance to help even a few
All human beings need your loving care
So we ask guidance from your kingdom up there

May coming together grant us all
Thoughts of service at your beckon call
Remind us of a maxim so true

"Do unto others as you would have
Them do unto you"

John E. Luckovich
Edmonds, WA

Something Better

Jesus made something
better out of me

Saved my soul and
set my spirit free

Turned my life around
Set my feet on
solid ground

Oh, Jesus made something
better out of me

My life was full of sin and
I had no peace within

Then I heard how
Jesus gave His life for me

With His blood He cleaneth me
deep within

Now I know
I've been born again

Oh, yes Jesus
made something
better out of me.

Doris Cox
Tunnel Hill, GA

I am a born-again Christian and I love to share Jesus Christ with everyone in songs and poems. Jesus lays these words on my heart. I pray people will see Christ in me. Not to honor me but to honor our Lord Jesus Christ. When we are saved by grace, Jesus changes our lives and makes something better out of us. John 3:16, 17 Rom. 323 Rom 5:8 To God be the glory.

Colorful Candies

Coconut, mango, grape, strawberry and kiwi
Along with maltose
And chocolate light color
Many red, green, yellow and white flavors
Tinkling my cherry tango
Twisting it with dancing fingers
My hometown
A vast, multi color of candies
Famous for its title
Bien Hoa-Dong Nai, Vietnam
My sweet birthplace
My floating baby sing-song cry
Never stop in my dreaming land

Lan Ngoc Le
Saint Paul, MN

Stop the Abuse

A child is brought into this world
To be cherished and to be loved
To grow up and to live
Not to be abused and killed
This world is evil and it doesn't have to be
Get your life together, and
Ask God to set you free
Mothers and fathers, you bring life to this world
Most of you are happy when a child is born
But you let your evil mind run wild, and then
Instead of loving them there is abuse and scorn
Children are supposed to be our future
So, take time out of your day
Give them a hug, love them
And listen to what they have to say!

Emma L. Hawthorne
Brownwood, TX

The Trees

How beautiful it is to look out my window
and see the dew shining on my roses.
    The freshness of the day started as I
listened to the birds in the trees.
    The bumblebees, the crickets, the little
jumping green frogs, all seem to harmonize
with the birds in the trees.
    Not to be outdone the ducks, the geese,
the turkeys near the pond sing along with
their own tunes warning them of danger
to get to the trees.
    The cattle, the horses, the sheep, the pigs, the
peacocks, the deer, the bears all playing in the woods.
    The squirrels, the owls, the eagles, and skunk
who never hides from the snakes. The snake
will snare its prey with poison, but the skunk
has his own perfume that makes the snake curl up
in a ball as he slowly slithers away to the
bushes and the trees.
    How mysterious life can be on farms,
cities, and towns, but even people seem to
enjoy animals, and ponds, bushes and
the trees!

Rhonda R. Carden
Moultrie, GA

Sister Sister

So fly, so sweet
Every day of the week...
You make a brother
light on his feet...
So fly, so sweet
How did we ever meet?
Was it accidental
or destiny's treat?
So fly, so sweet
Sister Sister
I know the streets,
I know the tweets...
Most brothers
just wanna creep
but in reality,
I just want a peep
of that lady
so fly and so sweet.

Rodney Peterson
Bedford, OH

May we one day truly love one another.

Beauty

Where beauty can be found
over, under, all around
Sometimes in the most unusual place
unaware that it is in front of your face
Many beautiful things can be found
Just open your eyes and look around

Cecilia Hattendorf
Apple Valley, CA

The World I Know

As the world I know confines her fist,
And I can't see past my fingertips,
To dim, dismal wilderness—
Darkness, darkness, darkness—
Into the shadows, into the night:
Barred from pleasant beams of light.

I turn; I toil and froth and boil,
Till it is but I, myself—
And solely myself—
That's still to know:
Until I want that, too, to go.

Shepard Harrington
Dallas, TX

Retirement Beauty

A vase with beautiful flowers
Is all we really need
To tell us we are special
To tell us we can leave

With all the memories of the past
And all those yet to come
Never thinking twice about
What could have been...or will become

A vase is meant to be refilled
With flowers bright and fair
To bring delight each day and year
As sweetness fills the air

Karen E. Leis
Wilton, WI

I Heard Jesus Say

Follow after me.
Create an environment of kindness.
Give of yourself to others
and show them goodness.

Base your reactions to others
with long suffering and patience.
Be careful with your reactions
and hold your tongue in silence.

I heard Jesus say to me,
"Use My holy word as your road map."
Lift up others in prayer
and stand in the gap.

If they ask you who to serve,
give them great advice today.
Lift up Jesus in your words,
so they can find the right narrow way.

Be the example that He has shown you.
Grant your neighbors mercy and grace.
If they don't return the same,
do right in any case.

Jesus is looking at you as His disciple.
Teach of His wonderful love.
Don't hesitate but speak boldly
of His gracious love from above.

I heard Jesus say follow after me.

Bonnie F. Tucker
Clarksburg, WV

The Wonders of Night

Have you ever sat and wondered
What a night really holds
When daylight fades
Darkness wraps you in its folds

A quarter moon sits overhead
Casting light, creating shadows
With underlying noises of things unseen
Making the blood run cold, deep in the marrow

An eerie feeling surrounds you
As a thousand unseen eyes stare
Every nerve begins tingling
What, with the night, do we share

The wistful call of the nightinggale
The hooting of the owl
Rustling noises of nocturnal beings
Sounds making you scowl

You see a movement that startles
Your eyes search for something not clearly seen
The skin begins to prickle
Other senses become heightened, more keen

As the sounds grow louder you begin to run
'Til you are safely inside your door
While leaning against it, catching your breath
You make a vow to venture no more

Laura P. Smith
Pinebluff, NC

Verona

Like a portal in a looking glass
its sheer curtain flows
Softly swaying hearts are praying
when the meadows in repose

Awakening on a greening mound
form pathways here and there
Sweetly refined so entwined
silk ribbons in her hair

Dressed in a gown of redbud
with pale, pink sleeves
Skirt is gleaming branches streaming
caught by a gentle breeze

Verona she's a daydream
verdant slope of emerald hue
So entrancing feet are dancing
could fly away into the blue

Swirling skirts and ornaments
bluebells sway beneath her feet
Arms embracing interfacing
moving to a heartfelt beat

Pink petals glisten in the sun
tender music lit on dew
Peace attending grace ascending
are such moments spent with you

Laurie Plymale
Carlisle, PA

Untitled

Sister and brothers,
Muslims and others.
Why do you think you are the only ones right?
Why do you think that you have the might
To impress your will,
How much ever ill,
Upon the rest of the world?
With hatred so hurled
At the innocent minors,
The ailing, nursing, blind and the signers.
Whatever religious beliefs you pursue,
You do not have the right to force me too,
To be of the same mind,
As people of your kind.
We are all the same,
In the Almighty's frame.
So work it out with your nemesis,
Who is right or who wrong is.
Two of you go into the desert,
Come back only if you bettered.
Your outlook on what is right, what is wrong.
Let the rest of us live in peace for everlong.

Jutta Janotha-Woitscheck
Vero Beach, FL

I am almost eighty-nine years young (ha ha) now. When I was born they did not tell my body it has to last eighty-eight years or more. I have lived thru World War II, communist Germany, and the good years in the USA as a legal immigrant. After my divorce from my American husband, I became a successful businesswoman and single mom. My most proud moment was in 1945 during the war when I saved my younger sister's life. During my life I had eight dogs. I used to ski in winter and swim in summer. I read a lot, travel often, and write poetry.

Small Print

I remember quite well
My dad a handshake giving
And today can still tell
Made deals that made our living.

Now deals are made like worms
And sometimes footnotes, too
That twist and turn to clarify
What each signer must do.

With many words and paragraphs
That sometimes cause confusion
And what they bring is not so clear
But to one signer illusion.

And in the midst you're often told
To get your attorney's say
The reason is the large print gives
And the small print takes away.

Carl Gerken
Roswell, NM

I wrote this poem in 2025.

Help Us! A Prayer Request to God

H - HELP - Help us find happiness, help others, be more, succeed, and maintain good healthy habits. Free us from pain.

E - ENCOURAGE - Encourage us to enjoy life. Give us energy to excel and inspire us to keep our eyes on You Lord.

L - LOVE - Teach us how to love ourselves and one another and how to appreciate life's beauty. Keep us from lacking any good thing.

P - PRAYER - Teach us how to pray. Protect us. Be patient with us. Teach us patience. Give us wisdom and guidance in all things.

U - UNDERSTAND - Give us understanding. Show us how to embrace you. Keep us safe. Encourage us. Make us mindful of Your goodness.

S - SALVATION - Save us, Lord. Deliver us from evil. Help us make necessary changes in our lives without fear. Free us from suffering.

Linda Beth Thomas
Aurora, CO

I chose this subject because so many people are scared and confused. The world is in turmoil. We need prayer. We need help. We need to ask the Lord for help. We need to pray.

Lie

In the Garden of Eden came the first lie
The Deceiver said, surely you will not die
The woman decided to give it a try
To the Garden of Eden, she said goodbye
A lie has the tendency to grow
Further and further from the original it will go
Where it comes to rest, we may never know
It creates havoc and a really big show
The lie a reputation will ruin
People accused of that not doing
Juicy gossip with mouths chewing
Imaginations in the mind brewing
Lies believed before the truth a way of life
Partial truths are malicious, deceptive, and anti-life
Lies are colored causing trouble and strife
Simple and selfish is the black lie creating lowlife
Fibs are lies of trivial matter especially from a child
Jocose lies are told in jest, a tall tale that is wild
Grey lies are hard to clarify, ambiguous and beguild
Whites lies avoid hurting someone and acceptably mild
Exaggerations are lies with fundamental truths within
Half-truths can be the whole truth with a deceiving end
Told big enough and long enough a lie will be the trend
Just remember the Great Deceiver is where lies begin

Bobby E. Hopper
Jemison, AL

Peace

There may not be peace on Earth
But you can have peace in your heart
First you must have peace with God
True peace quiets the heart
Don't let your heart be troubled or afraid
He'll give you peace in difficult times
Peace is our promise from God
He will give you strength
And bless you with peace
Out of a pure heart follows righteousness,
Faith, love, and peace when you call upon Him
Live in peace and the God of love
And peace will be with you
Trust in God and follow Him, He will give
You peace, His love for you will never cease

Madeline Carlson
Gothenburg, NE

In the Oracle's Chamber

Pythia sits upon her tripod stool,
in the depths of her inner chamber.
She awaits a vision, a future sight.

At her feet, the python lies coiled.
He awaits the vision with her.
He is her companion—no cause for fright.

In the corner lies an echo of the snake.
There sits a snakeskin, neatly coiled.
Not of concern—he has simply shed his old skin.

In Pythia's vision lies the answers snake seeks.
What will her second sight reveal?
When she is answered, snake's new life will begin.

And so it will be for you, you who have come to ask.
Pythia's cauldron holds many possibilities.
Many choices are given—which one will you take?

The future is simply yours to determine.
The direction you choose is where you will go.
So, pick wisely—the path is yours to make.

Robin Gerhardt-Linkens
Queensbury, NY

The snake, the python in particular, has always been associated with oracles. Their designation as Pythia reflects this. Snakes symbolize the process of transmutation. The morphing of one's form into a new design, as snake does every time he sheds his skin. At times we are also called to shed old skins and begin anew. And, though the future will always remain a mystery, we do have a hand in its creation.

Wall of Words

easy flowing style
defies most convention
when it matters
all about intention

in the moment
let's get real
is nothing sacred
that's the appeal

drain the swamp
many have said
release me from
tales of dread

quench your thirst
raise a glass
toast the faithful
devout the mass

just a thought
cyber free space
still the water
state of grace

Marc Miceli
Plymouth, MA

Whispers from the Darkness

From the shadows I heard whispers from the darkness.
A deep sultry voice calling to me like the wind.
I froze in a moment of time as I heard...
"What I really want to know is...
Just who do you really think you are?"
I quickly fled into the sanctuary of my mind.
I spent endless days and nights pondering the question.
My response...
I am everything you think I am.
I am the wind across your skin.
I am the fever deep inside.
I am pure, yet unclean.
I am the things you cannot see.
I am whole, yet empty.
I am the voice echoed in your mind.
I am truthful, yet everything you believe to be a lie.
I am the darkness deep inside.
I am the light there to guide.
I am everything beautiful you wish to see in yourself.
I am hidden across the skies.
I am the passion willing to survive.
I am the tiny ember burning inside you.
I am the flame igniting your passion.
I am you; you are me, and this is what I think I am.

Christy Schroeder
Canyon, TX

This poem is dedicated to those who find themselves questioning their very existence. You get to choose who you are going to be inside. I hope you choose to be the light that shines with strength and love within a world of darkness.

Connie Frenemies 2025

Frenemies I didn't know I had, so many enemies. They lie and have vengeance running through the blood of their eyes. I was like, oh well, I'm in my Connie zone. Can't you tell. They hate with no cause; they spread lies like a bad cold. I was like, oh no, it's both jealous man and female enemies. Frenemies stop using lies to get by, 'cause jail just might be your karma judgement. I was like, well, well, well. I was saying, oh my, my, my as I was waving goodbye. To all my frenemies 2025, the game has changed. Y'all know this song I am singing. Stop using lies as alibis. That group Envogue was singing.

Connie Abrams Gallimore
Knoxville, TN

Rome and America Part I

In 753 BC the kingdom of Rome was founded.
In 509 BC the Roman Republic was founded.
And after many fierce battles with her Greek masters,
In 27 BC Rome was declared an empire under Augustus.
Yet an obscure sect from a forgotten province
called Judaea grew mightier.
And in 313 AD Rome installed Constantine.
The empire split between East and West.
The West was ruled by Rome,
The East by Constantinople.
In 476 AD the West fell to Odoacer.
(To be continued)

Lewis Walling Findley
Port Wentworth, GA

O Children of Israel

O children of Israel, how soon you forget
The mercies of your God
Who delivered and sustains you
Through your wilderness travels abroad

O children of Israel, how quick to complain—
How thankless are your tongues!
Stop harking back to the chains of bondage
He has delivered you from

O children of Israel, we've crossed the Red Sea
But now we must ford the Jordan
To enter into our inheritance—
Let us rise early in the morning!

For greatly rewarded the people will be
Whose God is their citadel
And you shall remember the Lord your God,
O children of Israel

Markie Doczi
Middleport, OH

I am a Christian writer, author of Beneath the Old Oak Tree, Blue Heaven's Tent, and Sunday Thoughts: A Year of Finding God. I want to encourage God's people to keep the faith in these dark times. And if you don't know Jesus, He is waiting for you!

Come Together

I hear,
Noise of hatred and hostility
Echo throughout the vicinity
I hear mocking words that hurt
Within family, friends, and church

I witness,
Clergy speaks and spills his thoughts
Betraying God but he ignores
He voices his view to those in pews
Divides the faithful, drives out a few

I see,
Co-workers and teamsters
No longer team players
Now act like enemies
No productivity, no decency

I wish,
People could keep their views private
Respect family and friends instead
Let's make the world a better place
starting from home and our workplace.

Elizabeth C. Woodruff
Richmond Heights, OH

Death Comes A Calling

Anger and sorrow
rule the day when death
comes a calling.

Sleepless nights
and tear-filled days follow.

Life will never be
the same—tears can fall
anytime or place.

Only time will heal
the ravaged heart
after death comes a calling.

William E. Muehlmann
Midland, MI

Soul Survivors

Our young men and women
join the military.
Their goal is to protect
our freedom. Me, you and our
country.
You receive a letter
every two weeks or so. Then
the letters stop.
You hear a knock on the door,
Your heart and soul break. That
hurt will never heal.
Now, it is our job to continue
the fight.
Do the most you can to honor
those who chose to do this
because we are the soul survivors.

Edie Baker
Council Bluffs, IA

Kind Vs. Nice

Kind and nice are used interchangeably.
Kindness and niceness are not the same.
Nice is social.
Kind is character.
Nice is superficial.
Kind is compassion.
To be nice is to be polite.
To be kind is to show genuine care.
Being nice is surface level.
Being kind requires inner strength.
Holding the door for someone is nice.
Helping someone in need is kind.
People who are nice lack boundaries.
People who are kind set boundaries.
Nice is being liked by others.
Kind is being respected by others.
Kindness conquers all.

Ryan Christopher Warren
Longview, TX

Journal

Is there a poem in here?
Is there?
So many words strung together
to record events,
emotions.
Is it a road map of ideas?
Inspiration for the journey forward
Or
A quagmire of the past
to get lost in,
to grieve in.

Set it down,
    walk away.

Return to pour out more words,
thoughts rarely said to others.
Are there lessons to be learned here?
Is there a path forward?
Is there a poem in here?

Deborah Ward Hoglund
Youngsville, NC

Goodbye to a Friend

I am here to say a prayer for you
  a friend both tried and true.
Now you are gone and we're all sad—
  what will we all now do?

You got the call; God wanted you
  upstairs for other jobs.
We're still here shaken, but we try
  to smile between the sobs.

We now envision you in the
  heavenly choir that sings.
And flitting here and flitting there
  in your brand new wings.

Just know we miss you, love you;
  our loss is very clear.
And though we know you are now with him,
  in our hearts you are still here.

Tabitha Anne Yothers
Falls Church, VA

Becky

She left us her legacy
With needle and thread,
A quilt for the wall
And one for the bed.

A pile of scraps here
And more over there,
All ready to sew
Something pretty to share.

She left us too quickly,
Those she held near and dear
Are left with the memories
Of good times spent here.

And now we go on
With lessons she's given,
'Til we make our way
To meet her in heaven.

Marian Lenz
Forest City, IA

Sticky Fingers

She acted so hotsy totsy
Walking through the door
She sure was lovey dovey
Up to something for sure
I looked and said okey dokey
What's that up your sleeve
And let's not be wishy washy
The truth we all do believe
I want a teeny weeny drink
If you would all be so kind
With an itsy bitsy chip of ice
Then I'll say what's on my mind
I am not being a fuddy duddy
Scaring you out of your wits
But all is not so honky dory
There's things that are the pits
So away with all the dilly dally
There are those here that lie
I'll get right to the nitty gritty
And tell you all exactly why
My ring was missing holy moly
With that big expensive stone
Searched every nook and cranny
But that ring was surely gone
I am a hussy fussy and will atone
It's tit for tat his watch is gone

Marvin H. Hitzemann
Waterloo, IL

Simply Julean

It happened unexpectedly.
Quiet was the night absent of voice.
The moon eager to offer light to her reflection.
A beauty of her own doing perfectly flawed.
Candidly open to an offered smile.
Her eyes brown sugary sweet see me.
The warmth of her embrace creates an overwhelming depth.
An immense belonging holds the heart closer still.
I see her draped in subtle black befitting her choice.
She is the light in the room without question.
Envious stares watch every step.
My breath quickens as I feel her breath on my face.
My thirst quenched with a kiss her taste stops time.
In my arms hope is optimistically believed.
Simply because she sees something in me.
I flourish, she inspires more of who we are together.
Dahlias in hand we dance to our own music.
If this is our kind of love,
It's simply because of Julian.

Eric Lopez Fuller
Belle Vernon, PA

Aviation Tragedy: January 29, 2025

I sit here and cry
And wonder "Why?"

"Black Hawk down."
Did they have to drown?

Or was it a sudden loss?
Was it a sign of the cross?

A terrible mistake—
Pray for the Lord's sake.

May the skaters of "America" forever shine.
Those lives were lived extraordinarily fine.

The coaches, parents, friends,
The pilots, attendants—terror ends.

May the heartfelt distress of loved ones cease
And the dire questions be replaced by peace.

Joan Ball
Floral Park, NY

Harriet Tubman

She was the Moses of her day
She lead the slaves to freedom
She went from north to south and back
She told them all, *please come*
They traveled mostly in the dark
The North Star as their guide
And God was always with the group
Was always by her side
It was scary many times but still she persevered
For eight years, she never once gave up
Even though there were many tears
She led 300 to their safety, never losing one
She said her train never left the track
Whether under the moon or sun
With the starting of the Civil War
She was asked to be a scout
Her knowledge of the territory
Helped the Union Army travel about
She had such courage and so much faith
It was a boost to all the men
The knowledge she had of roots and herbs
Helped start them on the mend
She lived to see her premonition
Of the end of slavery
On January 1, 1863 President Lincoln
Said, "All slaves are now free!"

Pamela J. Yohn
Kokomo, IN

I live in Kokomo, IN. I have four children, two girls and two boys. I have eight grandkids and five great-grandkids. I have written poems since I was very young and gave them to people, but the last four years I have started reading them. Usually, my pastor gives me an idea for a poem to go with his message at least once a month for me to read to the church. My poem "Harriet Tubman" was written for a friend of mine who is an actress and was doing an impersonation of Harriet Tubman—what she did for the underground railroad.

Wishes

Here's to good wishes
Wrapped up in your heart
I wish you love
And all the happiness
Your heart can hold
Overflowing with joys
Big and small
May all your dreams come true
When you wish on those stars
May you always feel my love
No matter how far
For you will never walk alone
For I am right inside your heart
For when you love someone
We will never be apart
I love you
With all of my heart

Cheri Torbico
Howell, MI

To all I love, peace and joy, you will never walk alone.

Veteran

When their blood refuses to clot
and their hearts no longer beat,
they are laid to rest in honored plots
and their flag draped coffins are
carried down main streets.

Taps is played on a crisp clear morn,
while a bugler plays a song so forlorn.

Some had survived their campaigns
but had been treated by means less
than humane.

Some had returned home only to be
diagnosed with a myriad of syndromes.

Some lost themselves on the streets, only to
retreat into their minds. But lived by
the creed, "No Man Left Behind."

Some went on to be captains of industry.
Some became an amputee.
But all had one thing in common—
they all served with pride and dignity.

Glenn A. Powell
Winchester, KY

The First Thaw

The sun decided to stay.
Rushing water-diamonds in the spray.

Tulip and crocus stir unseen.
Winter's crusty coat yields green.

A robin fashions a pottery nest.
She's early, the sun knows best.

In the woods morel push up a stack.
Autumn's undoing and bends it back.

Bumblebees buzz the prickly gooseberry.
Fuzzy and plump they struggle to carry.

Until the ebony sentinel sings
And the pupa unfolds the wing.

The sun will continue the darkness fight.
The evening stars will call the night.

Tess J. Wilke
Durand, IL

Computer Bliss

Gawking and shopping on the internet store
If I time it just right, I can get in quick and score
Dozens of deals, dozens of buys
Anything I want right before my eyes
Just click on the item, it's yours in a flash
With all my credit cards who needs cash
Lots of items big and small
No reason to drive way out to the mall
I can shop in pajamas or whatever I please
Shopping at home is such a breeze
The hours are great, open all day and night
There's no problem if you don't get it right
Just ship it back, and you're off again
Wheeling and dealing for another great win

Judy Rasmussen
Twin Falls, ID

Soulmate

I need you
Here with me
More than the sun
Which warms my face
I need you
Here with me
More than the moon
Which lights my path
I need you
Here with me
More than the stars
Which number my universe
I need you
Here with me
More than my breath
Which gives me life
I need you
Here with me
Eternally
My forever love

Shelli Anne Adams
Christmas Valley, OR

Love

Love is a special gift
We all look forward to;
It makes us do some crazy things
We usually wouldn't do.
It makes us sing in a louder voice;
It makes us stand up tall.
It complicates the simple choice
When the decisions big or small.
We never seem to find our way
When love has left us blue.
We always walk in a silent daze
Till love comes shining through.
No matter whether you're alone
Or with your love so true,
Just give a sigh and thank the Lord
For the love that makes you, you!

Randy Klein
Spokane, WA

Awaken

The beauty of the Great Oak
can render one helpless
impressing upon one's soul
humbling to its greatness.

At winter's end, the music of spring
calls out to the Great Oak
"Awaken Oh Great One
from your restful slumber."

Share all your strengths
wisdom, longevity, determination
spread your mighty branches
give shelter to all who seek it.

A lifetime you have lived
thousands of years and still counting
multitudes of our children will live on
to tell generations of your fame.

Awaken to the music of Spring
to the warmth of the sun
to the sweet smells of life
Awaken!

Mary Marlene Daley
Roseburg, OR

Deadbeat Dad

Deadbeat dad
Heartache
15 years later
Loss
of a dream
Longing
for understanding
Hopes
of reconciliation
Realization
He is a coward

Kate Reinhardt
Newport Beach, CA

This poem is dedicated to my kids who at thirteen and nineteen came to be among the far too many who end up with an absent father. I love you for rising above it all.
—Mom

Autumn Leaves

It's autumn in all her glory.
Indeed a lovely sight to behold.
The trees are putting on a show
With leaves of red, yellow, and gold.

It nearly takes your breath away
Gazing at the leaves of every hue.
They seem to be framed by
The lovely October sky so blue.

One by one the pretty leaves
Come slowly fluttering down.
Each little leaf is looking for
It's own little spot on the ground.

They will form colorful piles
All around the naked trees,
As if to protect them from
A long chilly winter's freeze.

Elsie N. Kruse
Spring Green, WI

I Live

I live for the music, I live for the times
I live for the memories that bring words in rhyme.
I live not in foreboding life's daily grind,
When thoughts of my dear Lord Jesus comes to my mind.
I fear not the dark valleys of shadow and dread,
For He is with me as on I tread.
When evil lurks behind each stone, I know I am never alone,
For His rod and staff they comfort me and will lead me on
To a blessed eternity.
I pray each day for my family and friends, and hope in my
Heart they know our Lord Jesus is also their friend.

James Harwood
Spencer, WI

My inspiration for this poem comes from the times we let our memories of negative things that have happened in our lives, like heartache and sorrow, override the happy memories. I once heard someone say, "The best way to enjoy your senior years is with old friends, old books, and old wine." I want to thank my family and friends for encouraging me to keep writing. I was born April 21, 1946, was in the US Army from '66 to '68, and have six children and many grandchildren.

November 7, 2024

Every day should be a day of
Thanksgiving.

Every day should be a day of Thanksgiving.
We should remember,
not just the fourth Thursday of November!

In our lives we should thank God first,
the Creator of Heaven and Earth!

Remember, Jesus hung, bled and
died on Calvary
for you and for me!

The ultimate price He did pay;
we are thankful and grateful
He rose the third day!

Some, not all, take life so cavalier
instead of being thankful to still be here!

Please, less attitude—
show more gratitude!

Blessings, large or small—
be appreciative of them all!

So what do you say!
Let us be thankful and grateful every day!

Martha E. Kirkland
Hickory, NC

The Only Friend I Need

Friends may come and friends may go,
But there's a friend I'm sure you'd like to know.
He seeks me when I'm sad and I'm so very glad.
He's the only friend I need.

Through temptation or through pain,
His love shines down through darkened clouds of rain.
His holy word is there, cleansing sin, relieves despair.
He's the only friend I need.

There are the doubtful times,
The fearful times, the unanswered prayers.
This friend will take your hand. He'll understand.
He's faithful and true. He'll never leave you.
He is Love.

So, never doubt or ever fear;
He'll stay and guide you day by day, year by year.
Oh, to walk in His sweet grace.
One day, meet Him face to face.
The only Friend I need.

Melody Lynn Kunzli
Gainesville, FL

My Parkinson-ism

In my Parkinson-ism
I live there in prison

I write letters to you
But, the words are all scribbled
I drool and I dribble

Can't walk straight or run
Slowly but surely, I'll get things done
I have yet to see
The other symptoms that come over me

I have a healthcare team
That I have all seen
Through thick and through thin
I'm a survivor, all in

Think of me when I'm gone
I stand tested and tall
But I gave it my all

There's a better home wait'n
That's just for the take'n

Barbara L. Page
Two Harbors, MN

Fairy Tales

I'm living in a nightmare
No relief in sight
Feels like there is no air
There's now no reason to fight

There are no happy endings
Just living day to day
Knowing there's no depending
On anyone, no matter what they say

I don't believe in fairy tales
I don't believe in love
Only sadness and hate prevails
Never within reach, but just above

Latitia Mariner
Happy, TX

Our Guardian Angels

Even in the winter
Even in the midst of the storm
Somewhere up above the clouds
The sun shines the rainbow glows
Our "Heavenly Father" sends
Our Guardian Angels to watch over us
They guide us through the flowers dew
Their laughter is heard through the wind
As the birds fly among the trees
Their teardrops fall softly
Like clear crystal snowflakes
As they wrap their warmth around us
When we are suffering in pain
They whisper softly filling our heart
With peace and joy
In our heart they will always be
Even in the winter
Even in the midst of the storm
Our Angels are always watching over us
Psalms 91:11
For He shall give His angels
Charge over thee to keep
Thee in all thy ways

Frances Clawson
Newland, NC

The Way

The map is in print
Showing a new home
Requires making a choice
Two routes are shown.

The signs are clear
To guide to the right
One leads to paradise
The other to darkest night.

There are no shortcuts
Only the narrow route will do
There will be detours and ruts
The compass guides you through.

Having reached the end
What will you see?
A home in glory
Or eternal misery.

Sarah Bledsoe Pendergrass
Fayetteville, TN

I didn't have a poem ready and thought I'd pass this year, but the Holy Spirit kept prompting me to write. My challenge to others is to step out in faith and obey God's calling.

The Duck Pond on a Spring Afternoon: 2024

The duck pond today
A warm day, a gentle breeze
Scattered with its beauty
Of seaweed strewn in a careful
Symmetrical pattern across its
Silent waters, not a ripple.

Along its border are lined
The orange-gold day lilies,
And Queen Anne's lace.
And as if to welcome one, the
Chirping of birds sing sweetly.

Where are the duck? The geese?
I walk pleasurably along the
Edges of the duck pond, searching
And as if in answer to my quest
I hear "quack, quack," and
Afar off, along its outer edges,
There stand three—
One majestic in its coat of black and white,
And I am satisfied.

Olivia Serena Snead
Harleysville, PA

The duck pond ignites creativity on beautiful spring and summer days. This particular quiet morning spawned a completed poem. It also ignited a wish to perhaps write more poems created within this world of trails as well as the duck pond.

For Vice President Kamala Harris—2024 Presidential Campaign

With God's qualifications for your
Unexpected history-making presidency run
Of the United States superbly met.
Your due date was changed,
But your appointment promptly kept.

Lift others up.
Help others be free.
Your fundamental family
Truths were birthed
In you by your parents
And by your maternal ancestry.

Vice President Harris is our
Beautiful lotus flower.
Vice President Harris is our
Joyful warrior.
Vice President Harris is our
Coalition and community builder.
Vice President Harris is our
Trustee of democracy.
Vice President Harris is for
The people and freedom.

Jessie Epps
Whitmire, SC

Look Forward

I am humble
And I am strong
I look forward
And I go on

Yesterday when
I lost my direction
I stopped and
I moved on

Today I look forward
To achieve and
To move on
To move on

Tomorrow as I
Go on and on
Nothing nobody
To stop me

I am humble
And I am strong
I look forward
And I go on

James Fred Brinkman
Bismarck, ND

I live to be free, I write what I feel. Live on, be free.

Destination Heaven

Traveling down this road of life
With all its ups and downs
Someday I'll have my victory
And my soul will be Heavenbound

One day I'll leave this world behind
And labor here no more
I'll journey far beyond the stars
Through Heaven's open door

My palace it will be waiting for me
And I'll gladly enter within
The Lord will wash me white as snow
And cleanse me of every sin

The angels in Heaven will all rejoice
Another child has been reborn
Another soul has made it in
And reached their Heavenly home

My joy up there will be forever
I'll finally be at rest
No hills to climb nor burdens to bare
Just enjoying my God's best

Donald Mathis
Spartanburg, SC

Sunflower

She's like a sunflower you could say,
Standing tall, following the glow of the sun.
Her hair as delicate as the sunflower petals,
Soft to the touch, radiating beautiful colors.
Her love for life as full as the flower of seeds,
Dancing in the wind, rocking back and forth,
Calming the anxiety of the day.
And when darkness starts to fall upon her,
She will chase the brightness of life
Just as the sunflower chases the sun.

Nicole Lee Lowery
Trenton, TN

My Mistake!

I believed every word you said to me!
I trusted you!
How could I have been so fooled!?
So naïve!?
This entire time I believed we were on the same page!
How could I have been so blind?
So weak!?
You worked your charm so well!
You were only after one thing!
I forgive myself for my mistake!

Tricia Hope
Hurricane, UT

considered blue

when you see me, I'm drifting
I used to be a flower,
but things like that grow
the birds rising out of the field, north of a house
he rests for you
they loved each other, then you
the leaves 'my young friend'
spring, then fall, that of flowers, leaf, fields, or streets

children of the past, east of things, they used to go there
vivid were the plans
then you remember the seasons, south
it was colorful, vague the reasons, the things they did, west
summertime, place, ground just now, faint

Michael Metzger
Mooresville, IN

Things about me include thick and thin of life, along with facts such as I'm forty-nine years of age. I love spring especially where I live. It gives April and May an ere of green as the various shades come out and greet you. I come alive and stay that way by the work I do with my father. My mother is busiest of all it seems. Nature, my dog, good friends, and nice neighbors give me inspiration.

Sun Beam

Come sundown
Come stars up in the sky
Then the darkening
And the long cool night

Comes the quiet that is
The evening
A dog barking in the distance
The sounds of coyotes farther
still
Constellations literally passing
by
The coolness intensifies
False dawn jump starts
The birds
The vast sky with one
Morning star
Come the first rays of
The new day
Come the new day dawning

Lilly Whiteswan
Madrid, NM

Two Strangers Meet

Two strangers meet,
Two lives that crossed in the street.
Only too many dying embers
And too many lost Septembers
Had silenced the wind
That carried the songs
Of their youth.
Strangers they were not bound
By the seductions
Of each other's hearts,
Nor by the tears
That pulled people apart,
Gave way to the start
Of an everlasting friendship.

Robert Brooks
West Roxbury, MA

Don't Cry for Me My Children

Don't cry for me my children for I have gone away.
Those tears you shed in sorrow can never make me stay.
My love for you is eternal, but I just can't remain, this body that I live in,
lives in so much pain.
Don't cry for me my children for I have gone away to rest amongst the
heavens; but I'll see you all some day.
Smile and laugh in remembrance of all the days we've had.
Remember all the good times, forget about the bad.
I cannot take you with me for where I go today, to walk among the
heavens
to sing and dance and pray.
Don't cry for me, my children, for I have gone away.
I say goodbye with sorrow but I look ahead with joy to see the ones I love
waiting at the door.
Time for me is still now; all the pain has gone away.
Don't cry for me my children; I'm sorry I can't stay.

Willie Viola Bowden
Palmdale, CA

A Point of View

Sometimes it seems we just can't please
Some people whom we know.
No matter what we say or do,
Our efforts will not show.

Though try we may, it is in vain;
Approval would be nice.
But it won't come, don't hold your breath.
A closed mind is their vice.

For they have got their minds made up;
They keep us on the brink
Of telling them just what it takes
To make them really think.

Instead they've just decided that
They don't like what we do;
Perhaps they'll reconsider it
And see our point of view.

The lesson here is try your best
To keep an open mind,
And possibly you'll be impressed
And like just what you find!

Linda Mikula
Youngstown, OH

My poetry is normally uplifting and positive. However, I felt compelled to write this poem because I often see that people can be close-minded with their opinions. This can be very frustrating when a person is trying to convey a thought or idea to them. I have found that it is best to keep an open mind and value the input of others. We never know when it may open new possibilities.

Happy 57th Anniversary, Joyce

Happy Anniversary, my Love!
You are the light that lights up my life!
I couldn't have dreamed
of a more perfect wife!
My life's companion and soulmate,
I'll love you to infinity and beyond.
My dear, I've never regretted a day—
ours is the most perfect, marital bond.
So proud to call you my wife,
and so honored to walk by your side;
so elated to have you bear my name
and eternally grateful for your being my bride.
Fifty-seven years of marital bliss,
I would nary take back a day!
Through thick and thin you've always loved me—
Happy Anniversary!
Your kindness and love,
the joy you bring to my life,
here's to another year,
my most beautiful, forever, loving wife!
Here's wishing us the happiest anniversary
and for a love that grows stronger each year—
my soulmate for whom I'm forever grateful and
our loving, enduring, beautiful marriage my dear!

Richard Alfred Marschall
Melbourne, FL

Richard A. Marschall has written and published a total of eleven books and perhaps thousands of works of poetry, including four poetry anthologies of his own works. He writes in numerous literary anthologies and has published his works traditionally with Taylor and Seale Publishing, as well as self-published on KDP. Active in a number of literary associations, he has won the Edmund Skelling Poetry Award, placed in Poetry Nation's Poets of the Year three times, and placed in 1st position on numerous occasions on Poetry Soup. He was literary editor of the Scribblers 2018-19 and their president first part of 2020.

The Disparity of Woman's Suffrage

O blood bride
Whore of Babylon
Your pain cries out.
Whispers, even God hears.
Woman in white
Woman in black
Weeping widow
Oceans, the pools of your tears.
Alluring siren
Enchantress, huntress
Enticing, drawing me
Ever so slowly to the edge.
Jezebel, O temptress
Voluptuous vixen
Bloody, bruised, tossed
Yesterday's garbage, trash.
Squaw, welfare queen
Cat-lady royale
A travesty, the calumnies
Brought against you.
Suzy-homemaker
Gold-digger, nowhere girl
Infinitesimal, your body, soul
Our vassalage knows no autonomy.

Gabrielle Leva Nichols
Saginaw, MI

More Than a Mother

I do not see her, but another
in the photo on the stand—
my mother before she was my mother.

A singer, a lover,
a woman I could not understand,
I do not see her, but another.

Her laughter held a roaring hunger
for a life beyond her open hand—
my mother before she was my mother.

Her fading life pulls me nearer
to the fleeting moments we have left and
I do not see her, but another.

My whole life, I've known her,
but still, I misunderstand
my mother before she was my mother.

In her dying breath, I discover
as I hold her past like slipping sand,
I do not see her, but another—
my mother before she was my mother.

Jazmine Opdycke
McKee, KY

My Sunshine

Good morning
My Sunshine
The way you kiss me
It's the way you bring me to smile
The way I can melt
Like chocolate when I'm next to you
Smile like my favorite rose
With a voice of an angel on Christmas day
Kiss me with the lips of angel
Cherry red butterflies
I'm so lucky to have you as my girl
My falling angel of my dreams
My Sunshine, honey babe
Mondays you're my turbo shits
Tuesdays my boost
Wednesdays my delicious hazelnut
Thursdays dear you
Keep dear baby
You keep our love warm
Fridays my double-browed
Saturdays my legendary
Sundays babe you're my
Espresso shot for the day
That I enjoy all year long, can't
Live without, so rich
My sunshine that steaming hot
When I stand in your sunshine to keep
Me warm with your love
Seven days a week
The gifts on Christmas morning

Stephen J. Roberts
Troy, NY

Halloween

Trick and treat, or treat then trick.
Give me something to fill my dish.
Ghosts and goblins knocking on my door,
snatching up the candy I bought at the store.
All those sweets look really yummy.
But not too much, or it'll hurt my tummy.
Candy bars, lollipops, and gummy bears galore,
so many delicious snacks will have you
coming back for more.
Boys and girls of all shapes and sizes
dressed in costumes destined to win prizes.
From boys named Jack to girls named Jill,
look closely to see the headless horseman
charging up a hill.
Full moons, porch lights, and jack-o'-lanterns
brighten up the night.
Bats and witches on broomsticks out for a flight.
Frankenstein and ogres with a skin tone of green.
Skeletons and mummies in bandages will be seen.
Black cats and zombies out for a fight.
Werewolves and vampires looking for a bite.
A night of boos and "how do you do?"
What I'll get in my bucket, I haven't a clue.
But come to my door with a smile, no frown.
Or you'll get a rock like Charlie Brown.

Angela Sills
Cambridge, OH

I am going to be fifty-five years old in February. I'm a resident of Cambridge, OH. My hobbies include: writing poetry and short stories, drawing, crocheting, reading, and caring for my twelve-year-old Chihuahua, Taco. I got the inspiration to write this poem from my mother, Linda, and my former therapist, Lizzy. Both of whom are really big fans of Halloween. This is the eighth poem I've sent in for publication. I've had nine poems published in total as of today.

Stronger

I made a choice
A very long time ago,
Something I didn't want
That most do…

I lived my life my way,
Without consideration,
That all of it would change,
Someday…

Days, months turned to years,
Time passed,
As it always does,
Now the thought brings me to tears…

The chance to set the record straight,
The chance to want something that most do,
The chance to be someone I didn't think I could,
The chance to have a gift of our blessing.

But the days, months turned to years,
My choices have lead us to,
Weighing the only options now,
Our deep down, greatest fears…

We made a choice,
From this day forward
That our love is stronger
Because we are going to get through this together.

Deanna Willenbring
Kimball, MN

Silent Words

I will never hear the words
Grandma, Nana or Ruenan
I love you Ruenan
I love you Grandma
I will never hear the piddle paddle of little feet
I will never hear the cry for a need to be held in
My arms to give that special love that no one other than me
Can give
I will never smell that of a newborn, that our blood runs
Through for it has come to an end
I will never see the face for there will be not a trace to
Replace what has gone before
This road has come to an end
Never really thought about the words I would not hear
And now it has come to pass the things I will not see or hear
I need you Ruenan, I need you Grandma, I need you to baby come sit.
Silence

Larue Bonner
Brooklyn, NY

To Die

"I don't want to be old, I want to die," said the gentleman. His frame was thin, his hair more gray than not, but there in his face or maybe more in his eyes, there was something buried deep. He showed a loss of shine, his colors muted, both showing an emotional strain to be true.

By accepting his words your mind will trigger a response of how sad for him to say. Truly he doesn't mean he has lost all hope in living. That death is his only escape for him. Has he sank so low that life holds no meaning. That sunrises/sunsets, laughter of a small child, smell of coffee first thing in the morning, or a hug of a dear friend each have lost their enjoyment. Or most of all is there the loss of companionship/love of his lifelong spouse.

Days later I began to formulate another understanding of his words. Maybe, just maybe, he has accepted his passing as his reward for his life well spent, completed to the truest level. Wanting to put closure while walking upright, standing tall as he has spent his days. Days spent full of all the riches, successes, and fulfillment he managed. All in providing to his family. Not as an old man, sliding downhill daily, struggling not to be a burden to those who surround him.

Are these the things that make us who we are? Men who spend their days as the servant to the cause. Raising, putting on our "Superman Cape" charging out our door, taking on the challenges, to provide for our world. And then, way too soon the wall of age hits us square in the face: causing those around us to wonder why we have grown sad and melancholy.

To wish to rest in peace

David V. Raacke
Covington, LA

David Raacke, a seventy-nine-year-old veteran, retired project manager.

Inspired by Quote "...right and Wrong as the Same Color in a Different Light"— Where the Crawdads Sing by Delia Owens

The people of this world
Think to distinguish
Black and white
And the shades of gray
Think to distinguish
Day and night
And the light between
Think to distinguish
Right and wrong
And their mixed existences
By their standards
Are the same color
In the same light
But don't they know
Standards are not stone?
Black and white
And the shades of gray
Look very different
In the day and night
And the light between
Depending on where you stand
Right and wrong
And their mixed existences
Are the same color
Just in different light

Hannah Gregory
Lexington, NC

The Vail

A vail so fine it disappears between
    the rooms our soul does share.
In one our life from day to day
    before the world is on display.
Yet in the other so seldom seen
    NIE for but whom their vail was rent.
If through the vail a tear is closed,
    none but that individual ever knows.
A few sent back,
    their task not yet fulfilled.
Complete to represent or task insue.

Thus well aware this blessing not reward,
    but opportunity to go forth
    and introduce to the world.
The word well spent our sins repent,
    alas with faith, their vail, too,
    one day shall again be rent.

Note: NIE in Latin means Non Est Inventest. Or not ever seen or never seen.
    Rent in scriptures means torn or ripped.

Vaughn Carlson
Yerington, NV

*The indelible event of passing through death's door, only to return for the completion
of task yet unfulfilled.*

Ain't That a Shame

The difference between ain't and ant is I
I watched in awe as one by one
they laid their lives on the line
Each locked in a death grip
dying as the water
turned their world dark
Stretched across the liquid chasm
like links of a chain
Obedient pawns doing
what they were born to do
Laying a trail for the greater good
a bridge to the future
I laid a broken twig next to them
and watched others scurry across
Until there ain't no more ants

Rodger Cunningham
Atascosa, TX

I'm a multifaceted individual who writes, uses mechanical aptitude and creativity to repair, replace, and recover; the past, present and make my future. I believe in God, the Father, Christ, the Son and the Holy Spirit.

Peace in My Valley

I dream of a beautiful place where
my mind can be at ease

A lovely and wonderful place where
I can feel a tropical breeze

Where birds soar high above the
forest floor out towards the open sea

The pressure of life that plagues
mankind is very overwhelming indeed

They can disturb the peace and
tranquility of what the world should be

When things seem dark and dreary
and I'm searching for my spirit within me

I'll find the road and take a
stroll for peace in my valley

Kenneth M. Hurst
Allston, MA

She

A private person who walks proudly alone. So plentiful
is *she*, in her position of authority.
She attracts with assistance beyond limits. To please
someone, where something begins to happen. For
future time, *she* rests so easy. For her peace comes
as *she* silently works together with others today.

She provides the space to only begin again. To reach
that fabulous place of wealth. Yes, something of
wealth. Deep within her mind, with declaration and
assurance of a particular thing, while still being
morally good.

Eager, as *she* has expressed attitude. But brief
communication, losing her everlasting flow of time.
Time for peace. At the highest specified point, which
is possessing. To a person such as *she*.

Feeling the change and direction, *she* follows. Gives
her such feelings with intense and strong pleasure.
For *she* gives in to no one. Yet, still walks proudly
alone.

Cathy Ray
Lakeland, FL

Blue

Draped in blue,
you lay on my bed with cleats on.
The scent of your father's cologne
spills from your eye sockets, and
your shudders taste like salt. Your hand
goes through mine, and
I flinch—

stumbling onto a rusty swing-set,
soaring to the rhythm of the night we met—
your shrills of excitement
drag sandpaper against my body.

While my ears are stuffed
with honey, and my mouth spits up
cotton, I feel my vision succumbing to
your voice, offering another milkshake
to wash down the thrill of tomorrow.
You tell me to get breakfast; I grab fries to go.
They smell like the last time I saw you,
your savory first impression.
Even though you wore down my shudders, every single one.

You were in every moment—
I wish I never knew you—
spilling out my eye sockets, wearing my cleats,
going right through me.

Olivia Christina Mae Neri
Westampton, NJ

Olivia Neri, with the pen name "Olive," is a first-year college student and previously published poet with Eber & Wein. With this poem, they discuss themes of grief and loss through clashing sensory experiences that resonate in the memories of an unreliable narrator. Olive hopes to use their poetry to convey universal feelings through their own lens in a way that can be meaningful to any reader.

Don't Know Why

I do not know why our heavenly Father has secluded me.
Furthermore, He ordered His words put down.
However, you can believe this.
Time I have matured enough to listen. Tranquility enshrouds my soul.
My calm arrives with His presence. It sits with our Father! Hallelujah!

To those of us praying for attention, shout out...Hallelujah!
Glory to His holy name. As you can see words are many, for
I love you so much! I come and go as whispers! My heart never dies!
My kingdom to those that qualify is too much for your mind to conceive.

My blessings go far beyond any human conception. To those who will not
Be attentive to the scrolls, shall not be welcomed in my home.
I am being as forward as I will, for I truly love you that much!
Prepare yourselves! Glory! Glory! Glory! Glory! Glory! Hallelujah!

Marshall Thompson
Buffalo, NY

Home at Last

Here's a story with a splendid end
United Nations votes were aired
Listening to the radio in the living room
Abba counted the votes and marked in his book
I was awakened to *we now have a home!*
We heard cries of joy from the hall
I was eight and my parents took me out that night
To see the excitement with my own eyes
I shall never forget the crowds and the dancing
And remember it with joy everlasting
A state was born as we hoped for three thousand years
And I was there to witness it without fear
Wailing and crying and pain for those moments stopped
Everyone was swept into the emotions it brought
Shops gave out food and drink
Candy and chocolates scattered in the streets
Liquor, beer, and cakes were given free to all
And everyone wished it would never stop.
It is nearly seventy-seven years now and we are here
Living in this glorious country without fear
Sons and daughters are drafted to the army
To protect this wondrous country from calamity
We pray and hope the surrounding countries realize
That we must protect this country with our lives
No more living in fear and trepidation
Not knowing what will be our destination.

Naomi Kalisky-Jones
New York, NY

Prayer

at the foot of the hill
I am the tree
from the fold of the branch
I am the leaf
from the twine of the leaves
I am the nest
from the warmth of the nest
I am the egg
from the crack of the egg
I am the bird
from the wings of the bird
I am the sky
from the wild of the sky
I am all breath
deeply inhaling
I birth all that is, all that was
all that is to come

I am the hope
that this
is the right prayer

Rozann Kraus
Cambridge, MA

In gratitude I run, dance, swim, write, ride my bike every day. Those I love are near me and love me back; hence, this poem.

Life

Sometimes I wonder, sometimes I ponder
There must be a point to everything that exists
We are surrounded by people all in our midst
I find myself staring at people I don't know
Do they wonder about it all like I do so
We can't stop what's happening, out of our control
Learned it's better to just go with the flow
Don't worry, everything happens for a reason
So just sit back and enjoy every season
You may not always want what happens to you
It's all in His hands, so very true
The sadness, the happiness, the good, the strife
So just sit back and enjoy everything in your life

Frances Richter
Saint Louis, MO

Forest of Lost Dreams

Mists shroud borders as fog clouds the mind,
Ever in the gloaming no rays can you find,
Through the pall that would cover
As a dark cloak encircles,
Searching, you stumble blindly and seek to recover
The dreams you once dreamed of a future so fair.

Up in ashes with no flame,
Smoke lingers upon the stagnant air,
Sparks of hope rise to quickly burn,
Their embers falling to land in the loam.
Lighting flashes amidst thunderous refrain
To drown the cries and tears that remain
Unseen and unheard in this forest dark,
Unseen and unheard, do they exist at all?

No path to follow nor markers to guide,
Only a forest of dark trees stacked high to the sky.
Each ring a lost dream that has gone by the by,
Dreams that you dreamed of a future once bright,
Now construct the trees in your forest of blight.

Koneta J. Bailey
Hillsboro, OH

Congrats

Congrats to a life
Not fully lived
A life just begun
So much still to give
Not previously known
A best friend revealed
Separately prepared
His perfection shown
All for his purpose
We'll sing a new song
We'll dance a new dance
Divine destiny
Not by chance

Vasha R. Dickerson
Pickens, SC

Smudge

My cat Smudge
She is white and
very pretty, likes
to get into everything
Loves to lay on the bed
with me. She only
eats her cat food.
She plays with my
feet when I'm on
the bed, that's why
I love her so much.
Lays on my lap and
gives me love. My cat
Smudge.

Lorrie Ann West
Battle Creek, MI

Changes on the Earth

When God created the earth,
It was perfect in every way.
The only thing that changed it
Was mankind disobeyed.

The plants were green and never turned brown.
The moisture came from under the ground.
There was no rain and storms never came,
Just sunshine and moonshine on God's perfect terrain.

God told Adam don't eat from one tree.
Disobey and eat, death and changes you will see.
Being tempted by Satan, Adam and Eve ate
The fruit from the tree and discovered their fate.

Their sin nature spread through all of mankind,
Causing sickness and death on the earth for all time.
The whole planet and life on the earth changed,
Storms, flooding, fires and earthquakes in exchange.

The earth as it is was never God's plan.
Was completely changed by the sinning of man.
Will it ever return to God's perfect plan?
Yes, in God's time, and not in man's plan.

Marie Clark
Ballwin, MO

Life with You

I wouldn't mind
spending my time
living my life
with you.

I wouldn't care
being a pair
out in the world,
us two.

Timorie Payne
Syracuse, UT

Celestial Love

Let us meet
Where the sun's rays greet
The gaze of our eyes
And warm the depths
Of our hearts.

May the moonbeams
Sparkle among the stars
Dancing within our hearts
Assuring our love
Is never very far.

Kathleen Daley
North Tonawanda, NY

Snow Day

Snow
Flaking on the ground
Sunrise
As the sun sets
Moonlight
In a dark sky
Cloudy days
Snow

Flaking on the ground
Sunlight
In winter's time
Stormy weather
Clear skies
Starlight
In daylight

Snow
Flaking on the ground
Winter time's sunshine.

Audrianna Maree Hall
Myersville, MD

In my eighteen-acre yard it snows. That is what inspired this poem.

Moving On

The crack in the sidewalk
reminds me of you
of how I was with you
trying to be perfect
but noticeably failing

The discarded cigarette butt
brings back memories
of how you used to be
enraged, on fire
or nothing at all

The crack of the dry leaves
makes me jump
worried I'd turn
and see your face
ashamed, exhausted
a ghost of who you were

The puddle of rainwater
makes me stop
I stare at my reflection
unable to recognize
the eyes gazing back

I can still see your shadow

Skyler Alexa Metviner
Brookfield, CT

Behind the Curtain

I thought that you were here as my savior
But I forgot I was living in a fantasy world,
Wanting to be who you wanted,
Wanting you to be the one.
But I'm not that girl.
I'm not your girl.
I tried to get you to fix the thing you never broke.
Fill in pieces you didn't even know existed.
Get you to play the role you never auditioned for.
But you're not that guy.
And I'm not your girl.
And although it feels like this pain will never end.
We'll both keep existing in the real world.

Naiyanna Brown
Woodbridge, VA

That's Okay

As I'm reflecting upon all the things my life has shown me
I'm wondering why I had missed just one thing only

I always thought of myself as being independent
But then suddenly I realized those days had ended

And I haven't got a clue as to how I got this feeling
But I only know I've come to see what I've been needing

When you walked into my life, I said "Hey, that's okay now"
Your bright smile and your voice were so kind
That I knew you would stay on my mind

All at once I was enjoying moments filled with meaning
And it sometimes made me feel like I had been dreaming

While a part of me was still afraid of getting closer
I decided if you like me, that's okay
If you think that you could love me, that's okay
And then if I grow to love you, that's okay

Nina M. Beck
Redondo Beach, CA

I Am She

I am a woman who walks in style
I am a woman who speaks the lullaby and speaks in tongue
I am a woman who educates and motivates herself
I am a woman when I walk in a room I bring energy and shine like a star
I am a woman with multiple talents
I am a woman who has tears in her eyes with a smile
I am a woman who dances in her mind in silence
I am a woman of brown skin who came from a poor country but is rich in joy
I am a woman with flaws who makes fashion become noticeable with music
I am a woman who likes the color of the sea
I am a woman who will use her personal remote control and put you in
the ignore mode
I am a woman who has been josh on, stumbled, and has had calamity in
her life
I am a woman who sees sickness as a gift
I am a woman who takes negativity as a compliment
I am a powerless woman who dreams with her eyes open during daytime
I am a woman who plays an invisible instrument called the clarinet in
her heart
I am a woman who takes the word "NO" for next opportunity
I am a woman who plays ancient roulette with her brain
I am a woman who is unique, celebrates her individual daily
I am a Haitian woman
I am one of multiple kinds and
Yes I know I am gorge, short for the word "gorgeous"
I am a woman who says "Sak pa kontan an ba ke"
I am she I called myself Miss International, Miss Veve pronounced (Vee-
vee) not "Vévé" but my friend called me (Vévé)
I am a rose

Veldy Veve
Tampa, FL

Out of the Darkness

Sometimes I find peace,
and talk to my father.
When I listen,
I go farther.
8 years ago,
we were fighting.
Sometimes I think about the moments
that we parted.
That day is dark and yet the light
creeps in,
like days in which
we'd often laugh and move along.
Sometimes it's like it was a song.
But life isn't nice.
It sure ain't fair.
I think about us dancing at my wedding,
and you're not there.
Send us your love
day in and day out,
for peace
Is something to talk about.

Kayla Frances Hedges
Port Saint Lucie, FL

Kayla Hedges, Lawrence, KS—In memory of my father

The Final End

The end of the road
Each one that you took
The end of the story
Last page of a book

The end of a sunset
To darkness gives way
The end of each night
Sunshine brings its day

The end of the quarrel
No strength left to fight
The end of discussion
No more wrong or right

The end of one smile
Sad loss of its cheer
The end of the cry
With finishing tear

The end of your prayers
Each made with request
The end of a lifetime
No final regrets

The end of each memory
Brings the start of forgets
The end of a journey
You're history set.

Paul I. Lewis Sr.
Spring Hill, KS

There is a final end to everything we do in life, which makes what we do in life so much more valuable. The memories we leave behind for others to keep should honor us.

Happy 83rd Tenured Chapter of Life

Such a happy radiant and wise eighty-three soon to be
Yes, it shall be a luminous light on the journey just to see
Reaching out to make sure it is His will to be done
Embracing the expectation of grasping the tenacity of a prominent one

The mighty day of this wonderment eighty-three golden jubilee
Shall be a beacon of light to witness and see as an enduring clarity

What a blessing beyond the half-century in style for His Grace
Much visibility, wisdom, knowledge, and understanding is to be face

Eighty-three years of dreams and aspirations are duly pursued
Encompassed by every step on the path of the journey renewed
It is indeed a tapestry of love, faith, and might
Evenly woven in the breadth and depth of day and night

The inner recesses of my spirit speak out like streaming stars that gleam
As it reveals and translates the proof of countless dreams
Sprinkled with the congruency of the elements with the strobes of beams

Yes! This is a 'happy moment' of eighty-three soon to be
Thus a narrative proclamation is front and center yes! Just wait and see.

Yes! I would be remiss not to give rise to live, share much love, and not hate
No matter how hard those few who tried relentlessly to stop it all at the gate.

Steve Braxton
North Riverside, IL
The oldest of ten siblings grew up on an Antebellum plantation during the 1960s, picking cotton during the segregated Jim Crow Era living with mother and father in the Cane River area of Natchitoches Parish, LA. Due to the manacles of prejudice and racial discriminatory practices I did not get the chance to attend public school until I was ten years old. Nevertheless, graduated at number #1 and #2 respectively from junior high and high school senior class. After attending a couple years of college I joined the US Navy, reached the level of naval intelligence officer with top secret clearance, served in Vietnam, was exposed to Agent Orange, and was able to survive with God's mercy and grace.

How Many More?

Have you awoken and realized our existence is at war?
Our complacency withers them away; how many more?
If you were a tiny vessel, not yet poisoned by untruth
Would it be okay to take you and steal you of your youth?
Their innocent bodies ravished, then so easily ignored
Fragile shells tossed beyond the abyss of the floor
Their brittle heart racing as pain consumes their soul
How many more must perish before life becomes a goal
Thousands of innocent ones vanish from twisted theft
We still keep doing nothing knowing our child is next
How wide does this fowl river of blood have to flow?
Our hearts are tainted with crimson too if let this go
We have armies built for saving a rich man's wealth
Where is the help to save our youth from a horrid death?
How cold will we become to live these comfortable lies?
To what evil will we succumb, salvation we despise
We sold out our own tribes, snuffed out our own lives
When it stops being someone else, will anyone survive?
If you heard the screams of the innocence being lost
Would you try to save them and say it's worth the cost
Can we look them in the eye and push them into the fray
If we do nothing at all, we are incapable of shame
The signs are all around us, have we grown so numb?
It is too easy to flip a channel, what have we become?
Have we not realized yet that our souls are at war
We will all stand in judgment as one; how many more?

Marie Wilson
Shelby, NC

Statistics for 2024 show there were more than 49.6 million people in slavery, sold into sex trafficking, forced labor and soldiers. Over twelve million of them are children. There were eighty-eight million files reported to NCMEC. Human trafficking is the second most profitable illegal industry in the US. Reference: Human Trafficking Statistics and Facts. January 12, 2024.

Sweet Peace of Eternity

At last I have risen from the ailing fog
That drew me down its rocky road
And bid me to the of door of death
In my quaint humble abode.

How I did fight the dying of the light!
In the grip of hopeless despair
I flung myself at mercy's feet
And remained in fervent prayer.

All my strength was waning
And my bones writhed within.
For all that I now understand
I long but I had known then.

For I would not have fought so mighty
To elude this fate with all my dread
But sooner had I embraced solace instead
... until finally I was dead.
The sweet peace of eternity.

Bernice Bertolli
Lakewood, CO

I Am Blessed

I am blessed each and every day that is given to me.

I am blessed in so many ways that I can't count them all.

I am blessed with knowledge and love to share with others.

I am blessed to see to walk and to care for
others in their times of needs.

I am blessed with strength and health and
the ability to forgive when I need to.

I blessed just to be alive with good
health and wish I could be
blessed with peace too.

Gracie Lee Holman
Minneapolis, MN

I am Gracie Holman from Minneapolis, MN. I have written three books and I am working on a fourth one. I started writing late in life and published my first book at sixty years old.

Special Moon

Dear Moon: You listen to everything from me
My sorrow and my sadness
My happiness and my plea
When I speak to you, I feel your brightness

Every full moon you shine so bright
You give me hope and you give me luck
Thank you for every wish that has come to light
Every full moon you leave me moonstruck
My special moon I'll always see you shine bright

Amanda D. Perez Quijada
Bradenton, FL

The Forgotten

The wind whistles through bleached bones
In this forest they are as common as stones
No one remembers who those bones once were
Missing posters are attached to trees of fir
They are ripped and faded, the faces are gone
Whispers of names that are forgotten by dawn
The thicket is home to spirits who mourn
They cry for the past lives from which they were torn
The forest floor is dark and rotten
Haunted by the anguished souls of the forgotten

Roman Apollo Crouse
Reinholds, PA

Human Nature of Death

She watched him lie in his bed; his body was weak.
It was a late night in November; the weather was bleak.
He had lost his bright smile and began to fade;
She sat somberly by his side, sad, alone, and afraid.
Because he is leaving us, she feels extremely enraged;
As he continues the next life free, she remains caged.
His outgoing and joyous character lost its touch;
Now that he is gone she feels she lost her crutch.

Taylor Grace Waldeck
Lake Worth Beach, FL

Homeless

Her shoes and clothes were plain
but she looked like she might be in pain
standing on the city street
gaunt, as if she didn't eat
enough to keep her body going
and as the northern wind was blowing
she swayed with its effect
inside her head was a virtual wreck
from the thoughts that had started to accrue
because she didn't have a clue
about a way
that she could survive another day

Donald Gene Millner
Durham, NC

Different Times

Sometimes for work, sometimes for play,
they leave their babies most of the day.
No more twelve, maybe three,
they have time—they are free.

Just one spat—they are out,
back to the parent's home no doubt.
You wonder why they would not stay—
such a common thing today.

They could not leave their babies alone,
not many worked outside the home.
When they worked, it was tough;
they had no money it was rough.

With twelve babies, no going home,
parents could only feed their own.
Is this why the woman stayed—
years ago back in the day...

Linda Morrison
Tilden, IL

You Are My Salvation

I praise, honor and glorify God
You are my Father, my Savior
My Shepherd and my Prince of Faith
Peace, hope, love, joy and glory.

You are my strength and my courage
My dignity and my refuge
My calmness and my patience
Compassion, kindness and mercy.

You are my mighty rock, my anchor
My everything, but You dear God
Are my Salvation, and I humbly come
To You and ask You to forgive all my sins
And make a better person of me for You.

I love You, respect You, trust You
And thank You with all my heart
For everything You do for me
And trust my whole family to You,
God bless You all.

Esthela Maria Egeler
Oak Park, CA

My thanks to Eber & Wein for publishing my poems over the years. This will be my last one. I am turning ninety years old on May 19th of this year. I'd like to thank my husband Walter; my son Walter Jr.; my daughter Monica; her husband Alec; my granddaughters Macie and Lena; my daughter Sandra; her husband Steve; and grandsons Ethan and Brandon for all the love and care and for giving me a happy life. I am a very proud grandma; all attend a university. Macie and Ethan are graduating this year. God bless you all.

Whispers from Afar

I stand up strong on these two feet
Even though this world has got me beat
I know you see me trying
In reality I'm really dying
Giving myself a daily affirmation
But still not gaining any information
I fear that I am failing
Can't you hear my wailing
I try to keep my mind ajar
Just to hear your whispers from afar
Guide me in the right direction
Because based on my complexion
I am only facing rejection
Your whispers from afar
How I wish they were closer
And all of this could be over
Granny can you hear me
I still hold you dear to me
Your whispers from afar
They've become silent
And my mind is becoming violent
I'm giving it my all
And I'll continue to wait for your call
The only thing that keeps me going
Your whispers from afar

Brittany Jane Donato
Lakeland, FL

Skeletons

There's a skeleton in the closet
And a skeleton in the bed.
The secrets that you keep from me
Are running through my head.

Narrowed eyes with a glossy cover
And lips sealed with sticky glue.
Your heart beating with the desire
To share with me all that is true.

Emeli Rose Dion
Chester, NH

Life Not Mis-lived

Is there an easy way to endure the pain when your heart is broken?
I do not blame God for taking the person dear to my heart.

The sunrise I'm watching is quite inspiring. The rising golden rays give me
strength and the warming moves me to go on. I will find the love I lost, I
will love again.

Ah, what is life without the pain, to endure is to survive. When I go home,
I will watch the sunset before I sleep. The early dawn is a promise that the
sun will rise again, then and only then can I breathe with young heart,
new life so beautiful not mis-lived.

Aniceta P. Alcayaga
San Diego, CA

I Am Once in a Lifetime

To be here in this body writing this,
I've come to learn, is a gift in and of itself.
To be breathing, alive, lush with life, a magical
force pulsing through my veins, is a gift.
The chance to be who I am, the soul I am privileged
to inhabit for decades, is a gift.
To know and savor the fact that
I will never occupy this skin, this soft gentle voice,
this vibrating laughter, and this DNA
from my beautifully fleeting ancestry is a gift.
I will never be me again after the aging stops for good.
I will never know her again
in the most intimate, soul-wrenching ways,
and with complex love as I know her now.
When I pass into peace and dark I shall become another
and she may be familiar or she may simply have
the same emerald-wielding irises and nothing more.
I can only be the girl with the pointed nose,
full lips, mousey hair, and fair skin once.
I am once in a lifetime.
After today with her,
I can never get that today with her back.
I must spend every today with her until
my eyelids close for an everlasting time and
I cannot recall what body my soul loved so dearly
a lifetime ago.

Lydia Grizzle
Portland, OR

An Appreciativeness of Father and Son

Most come with thankfulness of this great surprise
At first sight sons are miracles in everyone's eyes
Explanations are what both must realize
For all sons view fathers as being wise
Because fathers view sons as being first prize
As time passes the confusion of love may be compromised
The son will usually view family ethics to his own size
Then sons are pushed into the world and take a ride
Into what fathers told them and it often is no alibi

Edward Larry Navarro
Copperas Cove, TX

Once in a While

Time goes by fast
Yet seems alone.
I miss you with each passing day.
How the clouds took the sun away!
Far away and a time alone.
When you're gone...
Somehow, I'd know.
Just as the sun shines clearly true,
I know I will again be with you.

Derek F. Walsh
Millis, MA

A sadness written in someone's eyes. All I can do is read, so I put pen to poetry. So we are less alone in the darkness.

Acorn

On my way
to visit her
but I

am feeling
just a bit
upset

I'll give her
a piece
of my mind

Then, I see
an acorn
by my shoe

On second thought,
I'll give her this
instead.

Aleksy Umbers
Woodinville, WA

Learning to Communicate Without Words

"A Man falls in love through his eyes, a woman through her ears."
-Woodrow Wyatt

We invented the shape of love,
forging it from the fires of our passion.
We gave it a name, but do not speak it
for fear of, in the summoning, it might lose its shape
or become lost in the intangible world beyond ours.

Danny Lee Brookhart
Scottsdale, AZ

If Only

When your day is not going right,
If only you could fast forward through it,
That would be nice.
If only you could rewind and erase
All your mistakes.
Pause or record special moments
To your heart's content.
Relive them over and over again.
If only life was a remote control
We could stop and change how it goes
But we have no say.
For our only button is play.

Kathy Renee Krzewinski
Chattanooga, TN

Exhale

Exhale in and out.
No matter how long the breaths last, they still hurt.
I wonder will this be my last breath?
Why does it hurt to breathe?
Breathing isn't supposed to hurt.
My heart is empty and in pain.
I want to build stronger walls to hide the pain.
Everyone I let in hurts me.
What did I do to let them go away?
I am tired of being alone.
Only my daughter keeps me going.
If I fade away, would anybody notice?
In time, I will be forgotten.
Will my daughter remember me?
Will she still love me or hate me?
Will God let me in or turn me away?
I just want to feel love and not wake up alone.
Who will hold me and take away the pain,
And say it will be alright?
Who will carry me?
Not to be selfish, I am tired of carrying others.

Jason J. Pruden
Sandy, OR

A Chair for Pop Pop

I know you won't be here.
It'll remain an empty chair.
I won't see your face in the crowd somewhere,
smiling at me as you hold back tears.
It's a moment I've imagined again and again.
If I could get just one more,
it would have to be for this.

I hope you'll be here.
I left your suit and tie for you,
right here on this chair.
A front row pew, like you would have wanted, too.
You can see the altar, but I can't see you.
You're somewhere better, I know it's true.
And I'm sure you couldn't have a better view.

I know you're here.
Maybe not sitting in that chair,
but watching everything from up there.
Smiling at me as you hold back tears.
This is a moment you've imagined again and again.
And I know if you could get just one more,
it would have to be for this.
So, I know you're here.

Hailey Nichole Metzger
Louisville, OH

Home Is No Place, But There's No Place Like Home

How nice it would be to have a flat driveway.
But the many fallen liters of grape and orange Faygo
lost on the hill in the battle of the grocery haul,
always serve a great laugh.

If only we had a garage devoid of clutter.
But how grateful we are to have packaged memories
and storage bins full of stories, so hard to let go.

Home, the most thankless job.

It is overflowing memories in every room.
Markings of many firsts and heights
engraved with blue masking tape and Sharpie
on the kitchen doorway.

It is each person identified by the sound
of their footsteps down the creaking stairs.

It is a scent so distinct,
never captured by any candle, laundry detergent,
or home-cooked meal combined.
Like a person's name you can never remember,
but a face you can never forget.

Home is no place, but there is no place like home.

Jaylen Marie Hoffmann
Pittsburgh, PA

Reprising the Stars

I thought this thought today,
but dare not say; too many words
may ruin a perfect day:

Deep thick miles of thunderclouds
Throwing flashes of lightning and ear-shattering sounds
Stubbornly conceal and obscure
These brilliant stars of ours.
When the weather gets this frightfully loud
Confusing and stirring this love of ours,
We must always remember what waits for us
Not far beyond these churning clouds.

R. Olaf Erich
Green Bay, WI

At Home

I set by a light with book in hand,
Yet I dream of a far-off place,
Where the sun shines so bright,
And the moon at night is a silver strand to light
  my way.

I walk afar in the quiet of night;
I am alone but not alone.
Yet no one is here, only a presence comforting
  my soul.
The moon no longer guides my path as hours have
  passed on this journey I seek.

The road has changed for my steps are light,
now a glimpse of the east horizon above the hills.
My steps quicken, my heart races,
the journey is nearly complete.

The sun's rays are appearing,
But wait...it is not the sun that gleams.
A city of gold rises from the darkness.
I am home!

Gerey Foskin
Yukon, OK

Talk to Me

Talk to me like I'm someone you love,
Don't turn away, don't let us fade.
Talk to me like I'm someone you cherish,
Let your eyes paint stories in my soul.

Talk to me like I'm someone you miss,
Like time is a thief, stealing you away.
Talk to me like my soul is your home,
Always belonging, never alone.

Talk to me like I'm someone you dream of,
Dancing with me under endless galaxies.
Talk to me like I'm someone you'll cry to,
A refuge when storms threaten your sky.

Talk to me like the world stands still,
Like love is the only thing that's real.
Talk to me, through thick and thin,
So our love echoes, again and again.

Talk to me like your heart beats in mine,
Two rhythms entwined, two lives combined.
Hold me, my love, and never let go.
Talk to me. Today. Tomorrow. Forevermore.

Rawan Bouvier
Houston, TX

Intertwined

Our bond intertwined
Almost as vines wrapped around the side of a tree.
Through each loop comes more memories,
Memories crumpled up like an old poem.
Ripping each unwanted page out of the book we've made of our memories.
One by one we fade away,
Losing what once was a story to tell.
Memories once flooded with emotion,
A hug once so powerful every noise seemed to dim.
Every light faded away.
Every breath was cherished.
Our love once intertwined
Almost as vines wrapped around the side of a tree.
With each loop flooded countless memories—
Memories we promised to tell our kids,
Memories to look back on,
Memories to miss,
Memories I will tell my kids.

Zofija Leocadia Koegl
Alden, NY

Meet Me at the Bend

where rocks greet the spring;
blue water, slick stones.

The light in the leaves, we'll swim
its breadth and back.

Take me to the bank.

The tide across our toes,
we'll lay in the grit.

I'll be your sunflower
if you'll be my roots;

hold me steady.

Tell me you love me
and I'll do the same.

We'll eat sandwiches
and pretend

there isn't work tomorrow
or the next.

Joyce Deuley
San Antonio, TX

Stardusted

She loved wild peaches
and had a fear of rain.
When the lightning struck,
it broke her open
and stardusted moonlight
filled her soul.

We forget.
We remember.
We die.
We live.
My muse,
it will be alright.

Kimberly Madura
Essex, VT

Healing

I used to rub salt
in the wounds you
left so I wouldn't
forget the pain you
caused.

I can't remember when
I last reached for
the salt. The wound is
healed, leaving only a faint
scar.

I'm forgetting you.

Ashley Gaines
Omak, WA

No Strings Attached

I just want to breathe
I want to feel free to speak my truth
Without worrying that I'll be judged
Or who's going to be hurt.
Because, man, I hurt, too.
I am human
And I need to feel heard
I want someone to care what I think for once,
To care about how I feel.
I'm always concerned about everyone else
And take on everyone else's problems but
Nobody turns to ask me, Hey,
What are you truly feeling or
How are you truly?
What are you going through?
Is there anything I can do for you?
...no strings attached.

Leslie Lee James
Tulsa, OK

Stay

Without you I shiver, my body betrays,
Drowning in longing, lost in the haze.
The closer I get, the deeper I fall,
Helplessly craving, I've lost all control.
I'm addicted to you, your laughter your gaze,
The warmth of your touch, the fire you raise.
You stir up a storm, a rush in my veins,
Flooding my soul with pleasure and pain.
My heart beats wild, my hands turn weak,
When you are near, I forget how to speak.
Every moment with you, intoxicating bliss,
A feverish high I can't resist.
Oh, let me stay in this beautiful trance,
Lost in your spell, caught in your dance.
No dose is enough, no cure will do,
I don't want sober, I just want you.

Amanda Engelberth
Schertz, TX

Death

Death is the most inevitable thing in life.
Some tempt it,
Some look for it,
Some play with it.
For me, death is sacred.
It is knowing that tomorrow isn't promised
And a goodbye not always rewarded.
It is knowing that today we breathe
And tomorrow we might be in the coroners.
Death becomes you when you least expect it.
It takes your loved ones when you're not ready.
Death the most inevitable thing in life.
It becomes you
And will become all of us.
It creeps in the corners, waiting for its next victim to strike.
You can't run from it.
You can't hide from it.
For if your name is written, it must take you with him
Without a goodbye or one last visit.
Death the most inevitable thing in life.

Yashira Cortes
Springfield, MA

Cleaning My Gutters

During the year, after the heavy rains,
the dead leaves are pulled off the trees
and piled with some rotted twigs
landing into the gutters of my home,
the gutters of my life.

Sometimes I can see the soggy soot
and branches begging to be yanked
out of the gutter to reach
their final destination,
the burial grounds beneath me.

The products of my gutters encircle me.
I take out my tallest ladder,
one of the many ladders I climb,
to get out of my life's gutters.
It is awkward and wobbly.

I try to balance, tossing my weight,
my pillows and cushions, around.
There's nobody to catch me if I fall
to the ground. I rely on my center.

I meditate and breathe,
    letting the ruins
        of the rains
            run past me.

Heidi Bellile
Streator, IL

This poem is about conquering the challenges in life to achieve a goal. It is a self-reflection of human vulnerability. It is about letting go of past mistakes and fears and moving forward to complete the task at hand. Heidi Bellile works as a therapist online. Her poems have been published in twenty magazines, journals, newspapers, and books.

The Spiral Staircase

Twisting and contorting the mind.
A spell that controlled many.
Intrigued to get closer
Kept at arm's length, at bay.

One step forward, two steps backward.
Chasing upward and downward.
When does this end?
Why must I chase?

The coyish game we play.
Childish are our actions.
Butterflies flutter through the veins, yet
Boredom and weariness take root.
Annoyance now sprouts... let's go.

The lost child within keeps the pace.
Afraid to enter once more.
Afraid to trust.
We do not let them in!

Outpacing the old.
Loving the chase.
Starts anew.
A smile draws the next.

Twisting and contorting the hearts of many.
Love is the burden carried.
Easier to stay hidden.
Keeping the blows to the heart...away.

Corey Shedd
Oneida, NY

Our culture has lost empathy and compassion. Loyalty is a thing of the past. Those of us left are like dogs chasing our tails. Love is our only hope to get us through these dark times.

Father's Motherland

Strip a thousand years of crown
Oak tree is my new ground, a new country
American robins lay loyalty
To gather twigs, moss, grass without a king
While Coronation Day, while tulips sing
Savannah's oaks sway not to sovereignty
Burn out the fire of sovereignty
Church bells toll the beauty of Jesus' crown
Westminster Abbey sing Britain's eclectic country
As pilgrims flee, save Jesus the King
Holy brotherhood found purity in loyalty
Home is deep roots and country
I will not scoff on Britain's king
He beckons Mother Earth's sovereignty
White swans, red roses to a king they sing
Hooray Blighty! keeps his loyalty
To old King James, where Jesus wears the crown
Red, white and blue fly in my home country
Also in Old England, where ancestors sing
Hooray Savannah! where oak tree is king
To brother to brother blood loyalty
To left wing fathers, who champion sovereignty
To American robins who nest tree's crown, we sing

Norma Suzanne Mahns
Pocahontas, AR

Basements Pt. 2

Because basements don't let you stay
And that's why, each night we departed
Ascending the stairs
Up to our beds, towards worries and cares
And each morning, just like the same
We were pulled back to the basement
Like it was calling by name
Until that morning
The morning they packed it in cardboard
Our basement in boxes
Then left it all empty
And like that we lost it
And we moved to a place where things felt mistaken
Stairs that went up, no hills or basements
And it's been such a long time
Since I've run down the stairs
Because there aren't basements, only worries and cares
Oh, what I would give during moments like now
To rewind the years and be barreling down
The stairs of nostalgia
To a childhood now ancient
And find myself company
In the embrace of the basement

Matthew Richard Moisant
Pooler, GA

Be Bold

Be bold
Be the first one to start dancing, the first to smile
Be the first to say, "Hey, we haven't talked in a while"

Be bold enough to finally say "I love you"
without a fear you won't make it through

Be the first to tell someone you're proud
and first to say "If you need to talk, I'm around"

Be bold enough to not fear love
Love with your heart on your sleeve
Love like there's nothing else you'd ever need

Be the first to laugh, laugh with everything in your chest
Laugh like nothing else matters yet

Be bold enough to live life feeling oh so free
Live like you'll never have to flee

Be the first to make a mistake
and keep going like you never felt it break

Be bold enough to be the one everyone wants to see
Be bold enough to be the one I want to be.

Carly E. Paine
Farmingdale, NY

The Reaper

Like a siren, he calls.
Like the darkness, he blinds.
Like a reaper, he takes
until there is no more.

The day I met the reaper,
I was in a cage
surrounded by the cacophony of my thoughts.
Yet he got through.

Further inward he crept
until nothing but him
was in my head,
taking control of me.

He then took me to his bed
and crept even further inward,
forcing himself inside,
covering up my cry.

The reaper took over me:
my body and my spirit.
The reaper will continue to reap
so beware of it.

Taylor Deters
Dunlap, IL

Purple

She wrote on the page in purple pen.
There's something intimate
about writing something quirky
about purple.
You can't buy a pack of
only purple pens.
It's picked from other odd colors
or the random one in the back of your desk.
She picked purple.

She wrote in my head in purple pen—
all in that lovely, lively, lavender color
It tinted our memories,
written in her words
in my head.

Pens run out of ink.
People realize they don't want to write in purple anymore.

Sydney Maree Weaber
Air Force Academy, CO

My Spirit My Soul

Sours higher with you
than without you
for you alone
have created me
and gave me life
for without you
there would be no me
Without you
I wouldn't have become a being
for you have given me life
an eternal flame
that abides from within
I ask of the Creator
give me what my soul
and spirit craves
for you alone
know everything about me
You are my Creator
You are my Father
You are my friend
and soul provider
Without you
there is no me

Kim Stallins
Homosassa Springs, FL

Blotted Vellum

I wish my life
was just another book—
a tome tucked and secreted away
among those shelves you love.
I would give anything
to let you peer into these pages,
to read my chapters laid bare.
If only you would pick me up.

I wish I could make you feel how they do—
my tattoos, the setting,
and my beating heart,
the quill that penned it all.
You could laugh at my typos,
rant about my loopholes
just for that one rising crescendo
to steal away your awe
and leave you bereft of breath.

And yet, you're stuck with your own stories,
leaving me to languish on dust-strewn self-promises
and half-hearted hellos.

Please.
Say something.

Joshua Michael Walther
Middleburgh, NY

Leave-sick

Homesick? No.
Leave-sick.

Stomach in knots, palms clammy,
Tear fogged, muscles tense.
Heart sank, chest hurts,
Share the back seat?
Give me your hand.

Stand in the rain for an extra hug,
Eye contact for reassurance and "It won't be too long"
Disdain for the coming emptiness.

Guttural statements... "I miss you already"
"Things are less fun without you"
"The house is always warmer with you in it"

Adjustment anxiety.
Flight booked.
Another countdown to return.

Home sick? No.
Leave-sick.

Bree Hendricks
Kokomo, IN

My name is Bree Hendricks, and I write poetry rooted in personal experiences—moments of joy, hardship, and the quiet ache of separation. This poem reflects on the longing that arises when your heart is split between two states. Each time I leave, I feel like I'm leaving a piece of myself behind. I use poetry as a way to reconcile that longing, capturing love and distance in words that bridge the space between.

The Victim

Head spinning counterclockwise, elbows raised
in defense; where's strength when you need it? Sweat
leaks from the walls as they breathe, faster and
faster and faster. Where's air when you need it?
Finger on the pulse of silence. "Please"—no pleading.

I killed someone. In my dream, I wrung their
neck and watched as a limp body fell. But
then the dream cut, and I hadn't killed them.
They lived, and I had a choice. To kill?

To kill meant to progress—but I didn't want to,
not like this. So I approached, palms
outstretched, ankles shaking, knees buckling,
but standing nonetheless, and said,
"Please, I'm not going to kill you."

But isn't that exactly what a killer would say?
And was I not already a killer, even if
my victim was still alive?

Julia Bochkarev
Oviedo, FL

Grief with God

You are so sad when loved ones pass and leave their
earthly home. Your sadness comes and stays within and
won't leave you alone. Remember God is always there;
He's just a prayer away. He knew this day would come;
He'll help you find your way.

And as a child of God, you know that it is true, that
Jesus Christ our Lord is watching over you. God
understands your sorrow; He sacrificed His Son. That
fateful day on Calvary, Jesus died for everyone.

He knew the time was here, that you'd have strength
enough, to carry this heavy burden, even when your path
gets rough. He'll be right there to catch you when you
stumble and you fall. And He will lift you up when
upon His name you call.

God knows how much your heart aches. He sees each tear
you cry. He will not forget you; He's right there by
your side. And from the heavenly Father comes comfort,
love, and peace. For He knows your sorrow, and He knows
your grief.

Cheryl Lynn Strait
Statesboro, GA

Stuck

Dear God,
I come to you today.
I need to feel your presence.
I need to know what you have to say.
I'm feeling stuck and all alone.
The trust and loyalty, I have shown
For nothing but my own.
What for?
I feel like I've been washed up on the shore,
Heart in pieces all over the floor.
So why try anymore?
What are we still doing this for?
I pray for a better tomorrow,
But lately it seems like nothing but sorrow.
Leaves me with nothing left to borrow.
That just makes me feel hollow.
So please, God, open a door.
Light my way like you have before.
Show me the light.
Help me find my fight.
Amen

Nichole E. Barnard
Jackson, MO

Auroral Reflections

Temporal archives exist in nature
That connect all existence

This is evident
As an early morning mist
Accents a tranquil beauty
On a smooth glass-like surface
Of a calm bay

A flock of seagulls
Emerge from this hazy mist
In fluid flight
Skimming the water's surface

The distant sound of a fog horn
Echoes through this cloudy vapor
Complimenting
An organic, scenic, serenity

Joining, uniting, and bonding

While highlighting
A serene inspirational
Eco-friendly presence

Gary Arthur
Hoquiam, WA

Shattered Reflection

A face in the mirror,
Yet not one I know,
Cracked down the center,
A web spun in woe.

Eyes hold the echoes
Of words left unsaid,
Ghosts in the silence,
Alive in the head.

But glass can be mended,
And wounds start to fade,
A fracture is proof
Of the battles I've braved.

The mirror still breaks,
Yet still, I remain,
Not whole, but still standing,
Not lost, but unchanged.

Michael Royzman
Mountainside, NJ

Can You Imagine?

Do you ever think back to the days of Just Dance?
When you would give so much of yourself—sweating, panting, face all red?
The days of Dad's pasta for lunch (he used to grate your Parmigiano)?
The days of colorful existence?
Of a world inside your head?
Of spacing out when grown-ups were talking (that's okay; you're only a kid)?
Of dreams so sublime you'd close your eyes and hope to find them again?
Because, though colorful, life's not that perfect outside your mind?
Because your first love,
you made him up while dreaming?
Because, despite yourself, you woke up (he left you, running, and he'll
never come back)?
Tuft of hair sticking out,
bedhead
(that's okay; you're only a kid)?
Of course you don't remember.
You smooth that tuft down now,
and that love you dreamt up
(rookie mistake)
is dead.
Because you just can't make things up like you used to.

Alessandra Kahn
Los Angeles, CA

Amoree You Are a Gift!

Thank you for being the gift
God called you to be!
Thank you for letting me see
what a free 16-year-old full of life and
ready to explore the world version of me looks like.

On our seemingly extra long car rides to school
you flood my ears with your 16-year-old problems—
from boys to dense people to things you think
you might want to be and do and the list goes on.
If you sounded like a movie
I would call you *The Never Ending Story*
because you always want to talk about something.

God said she is you!
All the questions are the same ones you had but
you didn't have safe ears and arms
to unload your world onto.
So, as you pour your world onto mine,
I know my face and expressions or lack thereof
scream, She doesn't care.
Oh but I do! This is a first for me, too!
So I'm just praying my way through because as you talk
God is showing me how to pray for you.
So please don't take my silence too personal.
I'm just trying to love you the same way God loved me!

Alegra Davis
Saint Paul, MN

I am just an instrument. Believe God!

Jolie

You weren't the first person in the room I saw.
Not because you aren't beautiful, not because
you don't light up the room—but because my
dim light never thought it was good enough to
look for someone like you.

But your light still drew me in and I was met
with the most beautiful soul I've yet to come
across. Oh the fools who hurt you, I smirk at
their loss. Fierce and bold yet elegant and soft.
My dim light never thought someone like you
could be in existence.

But to my surprise, I soon came to realize,
you're the only person I want to see in a room.
Eyes wandering, barely listening, hoping you
walk in the door. And then I feel it. Your shine.
Warmth flows through me striking me nerve
by nerve. Strong and bright yet calm and delight.
So here I am craving someone I'd never
thought I'd find.

Audrey Evans
McKinney, TX

The Internet

Internet, internet, internet
It is neither a fishing net
Nor a mosquito net
But it caught everyone in its net.
When the internet was invented
New ways to connect were created.
It changed the world very fast
As it influenced people a lot.
The handwritten letters vanished
And mails became diminished.
Emails became the norm
With everyone looking at the cam.
Living very far wasn't bad
As you could instantly talk to your dad.
But something bad started happening
As people's doors started closing.
Face-to-face talk decreased
As online messaging increased.
Everyone started typing
And alongside came down writing.
Although everyone seemed connected
They became socially disconnected.
But I am of the opinion
That we will all have a reunion.
We will all connect together
To make our world better.
Internet, internet, internet
It is neither a fishing net
Nor a mosquito net
But it is what connected our planet.

Shashwath Manjunath
Fremont, CA

I'm Not Sharin' Sharon

I'm not sharin' Sharon with anybody
'Cause she made me happy
Her I want to with other people share not
'Cause Sharon gave to me joy
Just like a toy
I need Sharon to be
Only for me
'Cause she was my favorite
Every place
Near Sharon I need to stay
'Cause she was okay
She would be better than a baron
Sharon, Sharon, Sharon
Be mine
Like a valentine
And Sherry wine

Sharon Millman
Far Rockaway, NY

Politics

Is red the color that pumps life through our veins,
or is it the hunger of heartless flames?
And blue, the hue of fresh air and clear skies,
or the thirst of winds that swallow our cries?

There are millions of shades between red and blue,
from roses to violets, blood to bruise.
Which filters of black, white, and infinite grays
will you see through at the end of your days?
Or will it be rosy, through glasses of pink
as you skate over pain far beneath the rink?

You sputter and shout;
you quarrel and pout
over one side or the other

of the coin you cast
into the wishing well of
my future,
not yours long past.
One face, an obstinate mule;
the other, a lumbering fool.

Your screeching deafens you to the cry of a friend.
Your opinions blind you to the smile of a stranger.
So now I implore you, when will it end?

Eliza Jane Spencer
Salt Lake City, UT

Unsolicited Advice

Given as a kindness,
Taken as a judgement,

I want to let these
Plastic pearls of wisdom
Dangle in the air,

Hover out in the open,
Never to be received,

Not to be stuffed away
In the stacks on stacks of such
Sage counsel already littering
The corner office in my mind palace,

A drab subdivision
In my otherwise plush villa
Where platitudes can be
Shoved away in an ugly cabinet,

While I'm down the hall,
Hidden in the lavish library
I lounge in to escape
The silliness of this conversation.

Kylie Witanra
Dallas, TX

When the Sunset

When the sunset
And I could admire the cotton candy skies
Even the ragged town of mine seemed to glow
For a brief moment, I am reminded
That if such monstrosities
Can look so stunning
Then at times
So can I

Ryley Ann Clarke
Peotone, IL

Rain

When you feel and get pain
Don't just sit around and complain
You know it's going to rain
Pull yourself together
And accept the terrible weather
Put on your rain gear
And have no fear
Walk, run, jump and have fun
Out in the rain, which has come
So, stop the compliant and have
A fun day in the rain
Along with that pain

Fran R. Bordonaro
Portland, CT

Campfire

The fire crackled and embers drifted into the night sky
No other light except the one I sit in front of
My eyes watch as the flames tango with each other
Capturing the beauty of their dance

As I sit in front of the fire
I feel the warmth of the flames
Lulling me to sleep
In the darkened forest

Olivia Katherine Wambeke
Altoona, IA

Animal Cruelty

Born from the womb to be slaughtered by the hands
Of an obstinate man,
With his ways unchanging, polluting our land.

To be ripped from her mother, with her disadvantage in size,
Held down to the table, a knife to her cries.

Chains to the throat and pains in her heart,
Slaved to the fields though glad to not be apart;
Millions of others: pigs, cows, chickens,
Crowded against splintering wood, all obeying their "part."

Shaylynn Elizabeth Herrell
Windsor, VT

Give Us This Day

The melodies create ache that echoes through my heart
I feel each beat, each pulse resonate through my soul
I feel the music pulling me in, engulfing me
And filling me with a hunger that cannot be satisfied

The emotion drawn from my being
Is heavy and pure
A feeling never felt before
Never to be felt again

Confusion and tension arising
Unsure of what this day will give to us
Passion-filled harmonies and fury-driven melodies
Blankets to the strong yet gentle voices underneath

Lost without guidance
Internal conflict buried within my bones
Tension growing, and growing, and growing
Then cut, suddenly, with a knife

Natalie Renee Koepp
Weatherford, TX

I Fell Harder

You fell first—
I fell harder.
What a cliché thing to say.

I fell for you—
You moved on.
My heart cried on your departure.

Now it's unrequited
But from a different side.
The line of our friendship has been drawn.

I've fallen for you—
You're not with me.
Forever, my love, I'll hide.

Trinity Kjelden
Bellevue, NE

Burnt Out

I forgot how to breathe
Emotions seeping from between
My fingers, making them numb
How could I be so dumb
To do this to me?
My hair is matted
As I begin to panic
The comb is tangled within
My hair and my hands
Have trouble to grasp
Have trouble to hold
To do what they are told
No, what they were made to do
But they have no clue
I try to get up
But the weight on my chest it won't lift off
So I lay
From day to the night
My life losing its light
I can't breathe

Ren Sexton
Menominee, MI

Darkness' Embrace

I can feel the warmth of happiness begin
to caress my body.
She whispers soft melodies of hope into my ear.
I embrace her hand and step into her warm glow.
I forgot what it felt like not to feel
the weight of the world on my shoulders,
or to not feel like my heart and mind are
constricting with pain.
The demons in my head allow me blissful silence.
The shades of torment have been
lifted off my mind and body.
The sun feels warmer, and the trees look greener.
But it all feels so unfamiliar, unknown, and scary.
The hope begins to fade into weariness.
The demons in my head beckon me back to the darkness.
They know I find comfort in the dark; it's all I know.
Waking up in the morning turns into a burden.
My reflection in the mirror becomes uglier.
Living feels bleak.
I start to descend into the darkness.
Any light is ripped away and thrown into the void.
I bid the light farewell,
knowing it will be long before I see her again.
I turn into darkness' embrace, letting it carry me
into the void of my broken being.

Madeline Wilson
Sayre, PA

The American Flag

The American flag means a great deal to me,
for it has always stood for freedom and for liberty!
For this reason we honor it and all it represents,
and we are always willing to stand in its defense.

Our flag of stars and stripes must never be rebuffed,
unless those who do it want to get really rough!
You see, "Old Glory" has weathered a storm or two,
and Americans understand all that it's been through.

So, everyone has learned that it should not be burned,
trampled on, spit upon, or generally spurned.
Yes, Americans take exception to any who act this way,
for our flag is red, white, and blue, without any gray!

So treat it respectfully and never intend offense,
unless you're really silly or simply quite dense.
For forgiveness can come to those who don't understand
but never to those whose disrespect is clearly planned.

When gazing at our flag, the best thing you can do
is salute it and treasure it unless you're a fool!
If you act in this way, then all should go really swell,
but if you don't, then things will likely not go so well!

Thomas S. Parish
Topeka, KS

Monster

Come one, come all, come gather around
Watch as she comes out of her den
Feel free to point and stare
Look at her dragon-like breath
And watch the oil drip down her face
Truly a monster-like creature
Look at the thing that sticks out from her arms and legs
Look at the bags in her eyes
Never truly aware of the laughs and faces she gets
As people judge her for their flaws
She wants to hide and run back to her cage
She's forced to stay for all to see
Her hurt and pain on display for your personal viewing
For this limited time only
Come see this monster we call a living human being

Emma K. Krug
Flagstaff, AZ

The Night

In the world of mysticism
you prayed for me

Come closer to me, reach me

I lie within your soul
You devote yourself... only a child

Helplessly you wonder

Will
Death
come for me?

or will the
night
come first?

And I answered you
on the winding path of my ghastly embrace

I turned some mankind evil, horrible

So much to have Death take your father away

I betrayed you

Natalie Kwon
Danville, CA

Masks

Smiling when you feel like frowning,
Laughing to conceal the crying.
Treading water to stop from drowning,
Not letting them see you dying.
Drinking to numb the pain,
Anything to make it through the day.
Hiding from the world so not to explain,
Why your misery is on full display.
Masks are worn to hide your hurt,
Can't let them see the truth.
The masks are meant to divert,
Designed to thoroughly confuse.
Can't let them see the real you,
Hiding from the whispers and judgment.
If only they knew what you had been through,
They might be the ones to offer encouragement.

Kristen Klapprodt
Meridian, ID

In the Desert I Wander

In the desert, I wander, going I know not where
Sun blazing hot, night cold as ice, sand among my toes
I wander endlessly trying, trying so very hard
To catch the vision dancing before me, I reach for it
Further away it moves, eluding me, taunting me
Denying me my heart's desire, what it is I am craving
I try as hard as I can, I cannot seem to
Lay my fingers upon what my heart desires
Is it because what I reach for is not meant for me
Is it futile for me to continue wandering forward
To decide what the value is in wanting something
Craving something I am not intended to have
Where is the worth in the time spent, the time loss
The journey made by my heart to a closed door
What is the reason to have to endure the pain
To feel the emptiness when want turns to despair
Is the journey of significance was the journey needed
Now facing the consequences, do I believe it was
Yes, I believe the journey was significant
Yes, I believe that the journey was needed
For each journey along the way, be it painful or not
Prepares me for the final journey that will lead
Me to the one that waits for me

Jacqueline Taylor
Cochranville, PA

Napping

Walking along
I'm quite tired I notice
Let's stop and take a nap
Lay down
On the gentle moss
A thick layer of translucent spiderwebs engulf me
Like a thick blanket
The radiant ferns create a verdant sky around me as they envelop me
It's then I notice it's begun to rain
But this doesn't bother me as the ferns serve as protection
Now I rest
Rest as the aching pines drop silken cones upon the carpeted forest floor
I dream then
Dream of cozy chamomile tea mornings with my love
It's after we've finished two cups that I wake
I stand and notice the rain is at a stand still
Watching as the remaining water droplets twist down spiderwebs caught
Like an ordinary fly
I inhale the newly rained scent and begin to walk again
Now I'm well rested

Charlie Sofia Monte
Eugene, OR

Lady of Peace

The Lady of Peace she was often called,
for her face was kind and fair.
Her conduct was quiet, and she was rarely appalled,
for when she was near, there was no despair.
She wore modest gowns that flowed in the breeze,
and a simple ribbon held back her long, golden hair.
Compassion and empathy came with ease,
for she was always ready and willing to share.

But her kindness was not limited to just those in need.
The knights, too, enjoyed her benevolence.
For she would often ride with them when they agreed,
until they reached a point of severance.
She was frequently held in high esteem,
for her eyes never showed contempt or malevolence.
It was as if she walked straight from a dream
when looking at all the evidence.
But it was always her faith in the God who can redeem
that made her grace and beauty prevalent.

Kaytelynn Farber
Bluefield, WV

Have Faith

When the sun goes down and darkness descends
When the stars come out and the work day ends
When the clouds drift by and the night breeze blows
When the memories return my heart knows
Life never again would be the same
As quiet spreads all across the land
Holding funeral programs in my hands, I try so hard to understand
As I think about the times we all had
While down each cheek roll warm stinging tears
I can't seem to bear the change
There is a time for each to be born
And when from you a loved one is torn
The harsh reality is hard to bear
Yet on your face there's a smile you wear
Unable to forget your sad heart breaks
There is also a time for each to die
As well as a time to laugh and cry
All the while knowing life must go on
Your heart shatters, for they are all gone
You must have faith, for what is
meant to be… will surely be.

Tiffany Star Cline
Durant, OK

Honey

I dubbed thee Honey
because in the Hebrew culture,
in teaching about God,
offer a taste of Honey.
Honey represents sweetness, abundance,
fertility, providing sustenance for our spirit.
God's word is sweeter than honey
Psalms 119:103.
Your kisses are desired
because your lips are like honey,
Song of Solomon 4:11.
Honey is the food God gives
to the love of His creation
Ezekiel 16:13.
Honey is the only food that doesn't spoil,
so your presence can never grow tiresome.
You are my Honey, I love you.

Ronnie Harmon
Temple, TX

Walk with Me Brother

Walk the well worn path of upright stones
A fearless tear for the names well honed
On more than granite and grave entombed

Polished white and guarded jealously
Walk proudly, fearless and lovingly
Knowing you are in good company

The markers mark more than songs unsung
They share this place with an unknown son
Walk somber, softly on paths well won

Thomas Dewitt Smith
Capistrano Beach, CA

Dedicated to: Randall Lee Erickson, Lieutenant Colonel USMC, Vietnam, infantry, Reserves 4/27/65–1/17/2003, Presidential Citation Award, father, law firm partner, Quote: "I survived eleven combat operations and spent the rest of my life trying to understand why I survived and the guy next to me did not."

Bleeding Heart

My skeleton is a cage for the wicked creature that is my dastardly heart
Trapping and confining it so my mind doesn't sway to its carnal hunger

And though the vicious organ of blood is objectively innocent and
untouched and untouching
I can't help but villainize it and keep it chained so it can poison me from
the inside out for its innate ability to make me feel

Because if it weren't under lock and key it would twist my conscience into
ripping it out and letting it free
Free to bleed its torturous hopes anywhere that light can touch and free to
spread its sanguinary desires where the shadows reign

But my shredded control remains and my heart is still confined inside me
And I am still filled with the red of blood and something that resembles
the remnants of love

So long as the nefarious being still beats inside of my hollowed chest
I am forced to rejoin the caliginous vessel of my mind and relive the
illusory pleasures and incessant plights of life

Sriya Potturi
Edina, MN

Redefined Reflections

Why is my reflection a whisper, so slight,
while theirs burn like constellations—fierce, alight?
Why do my features blur like ink in rain,
a face to be glanced at, never retained?

Because your light is not a blaze to blind,
but a steady ember, resolute in time.
Because beauty is not carved in a single design—
yours is endless, refusing to confine.

Then why do I reach, desperate, ashamed,
clawing at a version of me they might name?
I pull at my skin, redraw every line—
would I be enough if I made myself theirs, not mine?

Because the world sought to etch your name in stone,
to trace your essence through lines not your own.
But what you search for was never theirs to bestow—
it blooms in the silence where your true self grows.
I used to think so, too.
But beauty is not in the breaking—
it is in the unfolding, the rising, the embracing.
It is in the quiet strength that trembles inside,
in the storms we weather, the truths we hide.
Not in the limits they try to define,
but in the unyielding pulse of simply being mine.

Katie Le
Irvine, CA

Eden

The forbidden tree,
we once lived in harmony,
with our Creator.

Amaia Isabel Giral
Miami, FL

*Hi everyone, this is my second time publishing! I can't wait to read everyone's poems!
I thank my mother, father, and sister for their support.*

I Opened My Heart, but I Didn't Keep It That Way

We got along so well,
till we put up the walls.
I pretend like I like you,
till the facade falls.
Can you not
try to be nice?
Because I don't know that you hate me,
but I'd roll that dice.
I don't know what happened,
no really, I'm confused.
But I know what has to,
so should I call out the ruse you used?

Esha Suhag
Granite Bay, CA

Starlight Lover

Once, I was asked what type of "light" we would be.
You said I was like a sunbeam
and you were like a streetlamp.
But I see you like the stars.

Yes, a streetlamp is somewhat as mysterious as you,
but its rays give off a cold feel.
An eerie presence on fractured pavement.
A harsh glow that isn't quite real.
But you, my dear, are like stars!
Your warm radiance shines through the night.
Your intricate details captivate all onlookers.
Such a complex, yet beautiful sight.
Naturally admirable and perfectly placed
in the sky, just as in my life.
You have the courage to scale over mountaintops,
and you choose to spread joy during strife.
In a space that feels daunting and scary,
you bring comfort and feelings of home.
I look up to you like I look up to the stars,
feeling seen and completely known.
Oh you, my love, aren't a streetlamp, but stars!
An authentic and God-given light.
I can't help but to fall in love with you.
Such a complex and irreplaceable sight.

Madyson Louise Stewart
Rogersville, MO

Whispers in the Wind

Sway with me,
as the gentle whispers of the breeze tousle our hair,
whispering secrets of time-woven trees.

Serpentine vines brush our faces with their loving touch,
the rough bark of ancient oaks beneath our fingers.
You and I, rooted like weathered oaks,
aged beautifully like blushed wine,
our intertwined branches reaching for the sky.

Blades of tall grass sway,
changing with the rhythm of the seasons,
shedding our old selves, embracing renewal—
the fall of leaves: green, red, brown to bare.

In each cycle, we are reborn, our souls entwined,
blossoming from branch to earth.
I always fall for you, to rise and fall once more,
as the woodpecker's staccato rhythms
meld with the symphony of bird songs.

I remember the first time we danced in the rain,
our laughter mingling with the drops, twirling among the puddles.

Through the ebb and flow of time,
we stand united, weathering life's transformations,
our love as natural as light and shadow.

Our enduring connection, a beautiful scattering of petals—
a promise of renewal with each leaf that falls,
to be with you is to merge with the earth,
intertwined with the pulse of existence,
reflections of nature's undulating beauty.

Our laughter, whispers in the wind.

Lacy J. Caristi
Los Angeles, CA

Silent Tears

Alone, is how I feel
But there are no tears
I want to cry, I want to shout
Even though, nothing will come out

Alone I cry
Alone I shout
Alone is when my silent tears come out
Alone is where I let my emotions shout

Ghost-like tears, I let fall
So no one sees my pain at all
I stand tall, and smile, and laugh
When inside I'm breaking too much

My thoughts race
Filling me with pain
Never getting a break
From my never-ending silent tears

Jacqueline Marie Huffman
The Colony, TX

Light Switch

I took a drink I will forget about today
to turn on that light switch so I can be happy
Instead I feel a daze and lost my way
I search to find a way to not be so sappy
The days feel like a blur
It clears up on the first sip
People tell me I have a slur
but I am on a different ship
I feel my mind clear
my emotions are stable
I don't feel death is near
but I am not capable

I make choices I can't reverse
Do things that I will forget
but those on the other side of the converse
will pretend we never meet

I might lose it all
for the light inside of my bee
and trap myself inside of a caul
instead of letting the world free me

Alexandra Galaska
Pueblo, CO

The Shades Between Blue and True

The sun lingers a little longer,
makes you ponder.
Orange in hue,
shifting from a vast shade
of deep blue.
This hour,
incapable of blooming a flower,
draws a blade,
used not of harm,
there to aid
a glowing spade
to charm.
Sky of sullen black,
twinkles past their attack
provided by deep cracks.
Hiding in the shadows,
pink spread across the sky.
Dew drops,
mist,
open gliss.
Petals open,
lean to the sun
or even someone.

Kendal Layla Kay McNerney
Clare, MI

From a loved to more than my beloved. My friends who have helped me connect my stranded ends and straighten out my bends. You have led me through thick and thin, creating a path and helping clean up the aftermath. To that: I thank you, the ones I know, and the ones I don't. Thank you.

19

Reckless driver why did you hit him and take his life?
Why did you hit him and leave him to die?
Reckless driver you ruined the number 19 for me.

A number that used to represent the best days for me.
What used to be my jersey and lucky number.

Reckless driver why did you take him from me?
Making my lucky number be his day...
A number I'll never be able to look at the same.

My big cousin will never be able to breathe again.
My big cousin will never be able to see us again.
My big cousin will never be able to meet his baby girl.
My big cousin will never be able to hold her.

The number 19 will remind me of our family's loss.
The number 19 will remind me of those bad thoughts.

I will continue to grow.
And hope to see the number 19 in a better light.
Knowing God has taken him to see a beautiful sight.
Knowing God has him under his wings.
Knowing my big cousin is looking down at us being amazed.

Nakirah Star Bravo
Casselberry, FL

To my son Lucas, I hope you see my small accomplishments with writing and they inspire you to make your dreams come true—Mommy loves you. To my Love, thank you for supporting me and helping me through it all. Most importantly, my big cousin Nelson, we love and miss you dearly! We will continue to try and get you justice!

Forever

I think forever would sit
nicely on your hips,
nestled against the curve where my
fingertips and palms
find their place.

Forever—not as a word,
but as a weight,
gentle yet firm,
just beneath my connectors.

Where time loses its teeth,
its sharp, biting nature,
and all that's left is the
press of skin on skin.

It would settle there
without complaint,
as natural as breath
and conception.
I'd like that forever.

Neela Blue Bullock
Chandler, AZ

One Winter's Day

One winter's day
I sat in my bed and started to pray
I said to myself, Dear God Why
when all of a sudden I started to cry.
I said, "Why do people have to die?"
He said, "My child do not worry
just sit in one snowy day and watch the snow flurries
Then think of your deceased
and they will think of you with peace.
My child, go out and play
and I will talk to you another day."

Dawn A. Peterson
Long Valley, NJ

I wrote this poem when I lost my father from a brain aneurysm December 20, 1977, when I was eight years old.

The Color Pink

Lovely ribbons the color pink
were once tied in her hair!
The very shade that she loved best
she wore most everywhere!
Haylee's trademark had been the color pink
as we would watch her twirl—
one of three colors she looked best in.
We called her "our sweet pink baby girl!"
When she would choose a pretty dress—
"The pink one," she would say!
Besides the yellow and lime green
that looked best on her each day!
Her mom's then favorite color had been purple.
So she would occasionally wear that, too.
But Haylee was just the happiest
wearing pink outfits old and new!
Now, that color shall remind us
of the short years that she was here—
a little, sweet pink baby doll
we called "Our Best Four Years!"

Susan Truth
Hebron, IN

This poem was written in loving memory of Haylee Danyelle Mazzella. She was the four almost five-year-old daughter of Tommy Mazzella and Sonya Easley Mazzella. She lost her life weeks before her fifth birthday due to drowning. Haylee Mazzella July 13, 2001–June 3, 2006. She is the sister of Thomas Mazzella aka "Bubba."

The Movie and the Film

I sit and watch,
It's like my life is a movie, and I am the film reel
I cannot move, and I cannot change; I keep going.
The motions of every day, of all the monotony of weeks
They keep me on the path
They allow me to go about the days okay
But it's not! The world burns as I sit and watch
There's nothing to do; the helplessness ensues
All the shoulds exist but I cannot reach I cannot move
I sit and watch; I can't process my own movement
I hear all the well maybes, all the words coming at me
All deafened by the cries of the innocent
Deafened by the sounds of the very real bombs
I cry out, but I'm not heard
I look but the movie keeps playing
I sit and watch life go by
Consumed by these feelings
Life is the movie, I'm the film reel
My job is to play when pushed
But when does it end!? I watch the movie
I try to break free as it continues to consume me
As the media twists, as the videos turn, I try to see
What's in front of me I try to decipher
Reality from falsehood
But it's not possible
As my life is the movie, and I'm in the film.

Kaleigh Sohn
Pine Grove, PA

On October 7, 2023, all hell broke loose between Israel and Palestine. I was a sophomore in college and received this news, as well as the news that many of the people I knew and loved were lost or taken hostage. When I thought things couldn't get any worse, I was targeted for being a Jew and supporting Israel. I lived in my own version of hell throughout the following months until I left that school. I wrote this poem while I was sitting at work, processing everything and trying to remove myself from the situation.

Questions from a Shattered Home

What is love?
In my dramas it's so sweet and always seems to have me on the edge of my seat but that's not quite what I see. I grew up in a shattered household. Parents separated before I could read. Hate so deeply seeded you wonder if you're forced to choose sides in a war of despise. Forced to choose and mediate. The go between because they can't seem to communicate. Given twisted visions of the love and forced to envision if this is just some. Hoping and dreaming to have love like you see on the screens, but forced back to reality by the arguments between. Parents who can't get along long enough to be in the same room for moments in your life that feel like achievements to you. But what is love? I'd like to know the truth. 'Cause to a kid from a broken home, it feels there's no use. Love feels like a means to an end. Something that'll break as soon as it truly begins. I look around and see toxic behaviors and then… what happens to them all? They end up broken. Why would I put myself through that when I've seen it before? I know what'll happen, I don't need to settle a score. So what is love? I hear it's supposed be this great thing. But from what I've seen, it's no call for celebration. It's just a temptation. It will be over soon; there's no hesitation. So is this love I'm feeling or just admiration? It's so convoluted, I start to feel stupid. My feelings so lost from my broken delusion paired with disappointing illusions. So what is love? I need to find out what the truth is.

Olivia Nicole Sorgini
Columbus, OH

No One

What if the soil that my body
will one day become

is only measured by the weight
of the wrongs that I've done?

Would I be weightless or blameless?
Perhaps I'd be nameless.

Malana Lyn Recker
Madison, AL

Winter Solace

Bite of the arctic wind on unprotected skin
Pearl gray is the color of the sky
Storm clouds are soon to arrive
Lonely caws of a raven echo
A squirrel scurrying to beat Mother Nature's gift
Seeming like a blink of time
Snowflakes dance in the air
Trees are covered with a new blanket of white
All of nature is refreshed
Silence of my footfalls upon a white feathery down
Sounds of creaking tree branches laden with snow
Winter has finally arrived

Fern Gagnon
Biddeford, ME

Ribs

I sat in a strange symboled room, for pain
she questioned, knowing "You were two."
poking at my palm
a glass disc shuddered at her hip

Dark as the room, blinds seeping light
strange smoke drifted across her shoulders
My chest on the table laid, as was her
hand on it, reading, knowing
"Absorbed"
a more gentle word than most
"twin"
words as ribcages, the structures of secrets

The birds lacked chorus
"Two" as in one missing, as in not
where ribs go to be human, stolen
"Your pain is mourning."
My breath as in tin, as fools gold
stolen, I sat in a strange symboled room, for pain
she questioned, as the glass disc shuddered at her hip

Nicholas Heath Johnston
Kinderhook, NY

Driver

Body temperature on the rise
Heart trying to claw itself out
Mind jumping
Synapses breaking
Common sense dissolving
I've been shoved to the middle seat in the back of my control center
Firsthand glance at anxiety in the driver's seat
With its hand on the thigh of depression
It would be like my anxiety to not be able to drive alone
I couldn't take the wheel even if I wanted to
For the foreseeable future I'm stuck
Overwhelmed to the point of being lethargic
Holding my breath as we blow through our next red light

Carley Van Swol
Grand Haven, MI

This Moment in Time

A simple photo can show a lot
as a posed or a candid shot.

Each can glimpse an enlightened treat
of relationships that endured life's various feats!

So take a moment, admire its style;
this moment in time
will remain quite awhile!

Deborah Kammermann Kotecki
Branson, MO

Ancestral Destiny

Somewhere between the choices I had
and the decisions I made,
the path that I took
was already laid.
Though I was often alone
with the weight that I bore,
I felt shoulders of souls
who had been there before.
With no footprints to follow
there in the sand...
I'm still on their path—
by the lines in my hand.

Roberta Tynes
Ardmore, OK

Lovely Little Toy Animals

Little stuffed toy animals,
little bits of pretend,
sitting so serene,
surrounded by paper roses.
Whither did they come?
One from a caring sister,
     a dark, heavy bear orphan,
     a pert and cocky rabbit,
peeping unrabbitly around.
Two others, the gifts of caring friends.
These unlikely creatures
in an old woman's home
bring forth happy thoughts,
happy memories to one all alone.
All from many places, all to one brought,
All with a message of love,
All with a message of remembrances.
Lovely, little soft toy animals

Helen-Anne Keith
Chelsea, MA

I'm in my 105th year with my birthday in August coming up. My four girls and one son are now enjoying their diverse lives with all owning properties in this state (except for the youngest). She is a Floridian. The three oldest are retired. One has his own business and the youngest is still working. My hobbies: yoga, painting, going to senior center and Chelsea Yacht Club twice a week and, of course, poetry writing on communications to friends.

Wistful

I told you that I don't sleep prettily;
I toss and turn, I talk in riddles.
I've been known to shove people off the bed,
To kick, to drool.

You told me you don't sleep prettily either;
Sent me a picture, half off the couch,
Messy hair, mouth open, slightly swollen face.

"I don't sleep cutely,"
You captioned it.
On the contrary, you look tired, and sweet,
And all I want is to tuck in next to you.
(Even if that means I'm half off the couch, too.)

Emilie Wells
Carmel, IN

Broken Pieces

A heart once whole, now a puzzled remnant,
Looking back at a time when there was no resentment.
An abode, once home to two,
Now a soul left blue.
"Till death do us part."
To think that that was the start—
But no, that was the end,
As one soul began to ascend.
Only the fragments of a heart remain,
A joyous life stolen, a mournful pain.
I sit by your grave, reminiscing the past—
If only you'd outlast.
Our story, now told as caprices,
All that is left are broken pieces.

Anya Aggarwal
Montgomery, AL

I am a young poet and author who has published multiple poems and is working on a book. My dream since I was young was to be an author and I really hope that it will come true. I put as much effort in as I can for that to happen. I want to thank everyone who has made my dream come true thus far.

How Could I Stay?

Your fingertips pressed into skin
tearing at my flesh.
The carpet burns against my limbs,
I'm just grasping for a breath.
Bruise after bruise
from purplish-blue to yellowish-green.
Just wait a couple of weeks
and then they can't be seen.
Reflex, accident
all that's in between.
A couple of "I'm sorry's,"
one or two "I didn't mean..."
too much forgiveness for this kind of love,
a love that says it's never you, that it's always me.
You strip me down to nothing
showing me just how it's going to be.
Is it love,
or is it hate?
Whatever the case may be,
for an answer I can no longer wait.
You plead for me to stay
wondering how we ended up here.
Don't worry about that now,
just know I've cried my last tear.

Macy Marie Arias
Foley, AL

The Unknown Caller

Awaken from sleep.
What's that noise?
It's piercing the night—
One of the children's toys?
Made it to the door.
The smell of smoke.
I started to panic.
The alarm isn't broke.
The glow from upstairs.
I started to shout.
Please Dear God!
Just get the kids out.
Then the door opened.
The firemen came through.
Please save my children.
"Sir, they told us to get you!"
But who made the call?
Can't believe how fast they came.
"Sir, a call came in to dispatch,
But they don't know his name."
When I called out to God.
Did he hear my plea?
It was then that I knew
The unknown caller was He.

Jim Tanner
Pleasantville, TN

Daniel 3:25, "Look!" he answered, "I see four men loose, walking in the midst of the fire; and they are not hurt, and the form of the fourth is like the Son of God."

When Tears Fall

When tears fall
    there are things you do not see—
 how your words hurt,
    how they are haunting me.

I've done so much for you;
    I wanted the best.
I guess you didn't agree
    as you turned your back on me.

I gave you life, I gave you my all,
    the best that I could do.
As I watch you spin your lies of destruction
    the tears come pouring down
like the rain in a thunderstorm
    pounding harder and faster against the pane.

Harder and faster, the tears come,
    drowning me in the midst
of the pain that hurts me, that shoots me down,
    fast and furious, in a blitz.

I see I'm unwanted;
    for you, I will step away.
My hope for you
    is you don't experience
the pain that I've felt
    every single day.

Holly Grossenheider
Macks Creek, MO

Her Little Black Dress

Anna's black dress
full of memories
shaped the way she saw herself
She was confident in her dress, loved even
Images of her and James
dancing in the rain
captivated this cloth
One day that lovely feeling was swallowed

Dull and wretched the dress became, still full of memories
Sadness flooded her dress
Tear stains covered each sleeve
Wrinkles around her waist as if several arms had been around her
Grief had engulfed her
Mascara stained her cheeks
She was broken, overcome with sorrow
consumed by the loss of the only love she ever knew

Her funeral dress still on
reminded her of him
defeating her, tempting her
telling her that it will all go away with just one taste
Escaping from her memories
she tasted the bittersweet drink, over and over
until she felt nothing, nothing at all

Hannah Leigh Green
Siloam Springs, AR

Extra Chromosome

He was a premie
Spent weeks in the NICU
He has an extra chromosome
He is mute
Like a detective, he figures out
how to unlock and open anything
To his family he is king
Eating snacks is his vice
He likes to ask for cheeseballs
On his ACC device
He teaches us to be inclusive
Shouldn't that be a world goal?
No excuses!

Terri Ricardo
Massachusetts

Haunted by Fate

Innocent hearts, misunderstood.
Oh, what a moment it was,
as two souls spontaneously entwined.
You walked me through open plains and guided me
through the thickest mud.
Showed me that a friendship can grow like a weed
in unforeseen places.
Yet, this simple love could only be seen by us,
hidden like a treasure in the deepest sea.
Limited in our places, inadequate to be, still we grew.
And as we grew, we flew.
Drifting apart, I wondered if I'd ever see you again.
Yet, you always return as a simple reminder
with that soft smile.
That simple love is only stronger until we ponder.
A love so pure and young, lost but never forgotten.
A piece of you will always reside in my heart,
forever tangled within my soul.

Grace Marie Wade
Hereford, TX

Struggles

You like to smile at me
Make pleasantries
But do you ever really notice me

Do you ever see the scars
The ones that cover my skin
Do you ever notice my pain
All the ways it seeps in

I lie and say I'm sick
When I'm really just at home
I tell people I'm okay
Yet I struggle through the day

It's hard being a teen girl
Least it is for me
So much pressure all the time
Everyone's into getting high

I'm sick and I'm tired
Of lying through my teeth
Free me from all this pressure
I'm done let me be

Kaitlyn Wilmot
Hopewell, NJ

Maturity

It's 25 degrees outside and
I've got two things on my mind.
What do I have for breakfast tomorrow
and what is the meaning of life?
When you can't choose who stays and who goes
what is the point of loving?
When the lines between bad and good blur
what makes me different from the others?
The days melt from one to another;
it's been a week, no a month
oh god a year
and I still have none of the power.

Kiera Jasmine Walker
Darby, MT

Loose Change

I can't afford to be up pondering
It's expensive, costly
Exchanging the words brought from me

But the truth is I'd spend every loose penny on you
My spare change finally coming to use
You, only you, my favorite muse

Hallie Mae Davis
McCordsville, IN

Homeless

It happens every night and every day.
You've got nowhere to go or nowhere
to stay. You're homeless and that's the
saddest way. You roam the street,
and asking for money to get something
to eat. You'll sleep in cars or vans
or on land. Sleeping on park benches
all day and all night or on the ground
till the morning light. And when you
lose your job, your home, your child,
and your wife you'll be homeless for the
rest of your life.

Emily Davis
Petersburg, VA

In the Quiet Darkness of the Night

Oh, how inspiring is the nature
in the long daytime of light
and quiet darkness of the night
Taking shelter
or giving shelter
it is all a state of living
the nature of what matters

Teach the young
when taking flight
to do with all their might
To feel every flap and lift
the current and wind against
the stretched tip of feathers
and know how inspiring is the nature…

The world is theirs
to capture the moments
to see the beauty
of the world beyond
Make it better for one and all
That's the reason we are born
Nature teaches us every morn

Every moment is worth living
Every morning is worth awaking!

Veeraramani S. Rajaratnam
Franklin, TN

A scientist-turned-poet and a doctorate from Marquette University, WI, I was born and raised in Ceylon (now Sri Lanka). Traveling halfway across the world, I have lived and taught in Sri Lanka, Nigeria, and at medical schools in the US. I have always loved teaching youngsters including my own children and grandchildren and aspire to make them appreciate 'nature and the blessings abound' to joyfully strive beyond the daily challenges in life. This poem titled "In the Quiet Darkness of the Night" shares my aspiration for the young to embrace life completely, seeking, in awe, the joy nature brings.

Paradigm Shift

It is about time
We rethink the paradigm
Surrounding Son of Man.
From victim to victor,
Conquered to conqueror,
Hunted to hunter, and
Lamb to roaring lion.
He hunkered and patiently
Waited to ensnare the enemy
Whose extravagance and arrogance
Made him an easy prey,
Unable to see the truth—
Divine essence hidden
In human cloak; for once,
Deceiver was deceived.
Son of Man on the cross as bait,
The enemy started to celebrate.
With the stillness of a predator
The Son of Man pounced on Satan
In the middle of his victory dance,
Astounded when ambushed
And devoured...
The Son of God ascended
The golden stairs
Amid hallelujahs and cheers.

Melinda Montilla
Canton, MI

Songbird

Oh sweet songbird, sing for them your golden symphony,
Draw forth from the masses their misty-eyed sympathy,
Rejoice among them! Mere bars isolate from festivity.

Oh sweet songbird, recall for them your silver songs.
As soul flows from brazen break, love will be lifelong.
Never stop, lest those gnawing thoughts if you belong.

Oh sweet songbird, force for them your bronze melodies;
Those glitzy affairs drew venomous ire and jealousy,
Sweet tones filled to the brim with melancholy elegies.

Oh sweet songbird, save for yourself that tinny tune;
Let dulcet notes mingle within nature's sweet croon,
Reclaim antiquated cadences and new love you'll swoon.

Lilly Desdemona
Port Orange, FL

This Little Blight of Mine

It tightens its leash and drags me around
Hate churns in my gut, for it is my bane
If I swim for the surface it drags me down

It sours my brain
Blurs my sight
For all of my woes, it is to blame

It clings to me like a pulsing blight
It's only silent when I relapse again
Just one more time wouldn't hurt, right?

Kyrus Epton Scott
Tupelo, MS

Told you.

To Be Free

When the riptide denies its course of time,
strike a war through my veins.
So if death kills me,
I will sing a song of grace and fall as softly as I've been made.
Sunday morning you undid the latch to my soul.
Are your secrets made of my shame,
and lust, and unrequited love?
Two can be made the same when
you weave and sew from a grave.
And so I ask, the hunger of survival
is disarming to you, isn't it?
The rush, the pray, a touch, a say;
the guilt, the gun, the disarray.
Love is made with so much pain.
An alluring look is all it takes
to dismantle the morality in you.
Do understand, discovery will
sullen your soul bare and bleak.

As you notice the wave which washes weary,
do you see where sky meets sea?
Let the ocean be your savior,
let the sky show you grace.
For this is the way into peace,
the only way, to be free.

Samantha Garcia
Allen, TX

"I Love You"

The words "I love you" hold such meaning;
it's difficult for me to spit them out.
They can't understand why I don't reply
because to them, it's just another phrase.

For me, it's much more, deep and heavy.
As of now, I'm not sure I feel ready.
And so, my gratitude stays unexpressed.
Maybe one day I'll get this off my chest.

Dominika Wojciechowska
Key West, FL

Acceptance

All my life I wanted my mother to like me;
When I was younger I tried to be all she wanted me to be.
I've always known she liked my brother the best.
I could never seem to pass her test.
Now I'm much older but some things never change;
Vying for acceptance is out of my range.
Her health is now failing so very, very fast.
Sometimes I look at her and think she can't last.
I've always loved my mother
Although she makes me feel she wishes
I was another!

Maggie Flanigan
Sun City Center, FL

Our New Year "2025"

Yearly holidays have come and gone! We enjoyed
family and friends togetherness with blessings
of foods and holiday songs. Now the "2025"
winter snows have been setting in. Snow and
coldness have affected the nation. I get a lot of mail—some
political, religious, and such! It makes me think
of personal prayers needed so much. We the
people and our leaders need God's touch! In
years gone by teens enjoyed weekly Bible studies
of games and it was such fun! It seems the world
goes through too much anymore! I recall the
elderly teachings and others, too... (Forgiveness is so
hard to do.) But bitterness has got to go. This is
important that even leaders should know!

Frances Elaine Camp
Americus, GA

The book Willow Grove Lane *I've authored is to be offered to TV, film, movie, possibly before too long. I hope for the miracle of it. I have been notified twice concerning it. My name and story title was recommended to someone in another state that it's a good story!*

I Am From

I am from Clarinet
From Mossy Oak and Realtree
I am from Ivy, growing up with me
I'm from blonde hair and blue eyes
From Catherine and Jackson
I'm from the Russells and the Greens
From "You get what you get and you don't throw a fit"
I'm from Maine
I'm from the tall, discolored house on Townhouse Road
From it-took-four-years-to-build-our-dream-house
From Meme and Papa
From Grandma and Toddly
From Nini and Grampie
I'm from all my parents loving me unconditionally
I'm from the late-night Dairy Queen trips with my mom
And early morning Dunkin trips with my dad
From Alexia's and Pizza Gourmet
From Kancamagas Highway in the August heat
I'm from Waldo County
I'm from sleepovers with my mom and her friends
From Bath and Body Works and the Bangor Mall
I'm from the overwhelming but comfortable heat of the woodstove
I'm from my family

Kaylie Ann Green
Lincolnville, ME

Hi, I'm Kaylie Green, named after my great-grandmother Catherine. I was born on October 24, 2011. I have two siblings: Vanessa my stepsister is thirteen, always has the best advice, and is my best friend, while my half brother Brody is two and the highlight of my every day. 2025 is my second year going to districts for band. I play clarinet for my school. I love shopping and spending time with my family and friends. My poem was a written piece for English class based on the poem by George Ella Lyon.

Hug

Softly I fall as tension crawls
    Into open arms where silence calls
A frozen space, our hearts align
    In this gentle bond, all worries decline
Warmth envelops, a sheltering sigh
    In this embrace, the world drifts by
Time stands still, in a tender hold
    A moment of solace, a story retold
Whispers of comfort breath to breath
    In the hush of love, we conquer death
Here, in this hug, we find our peace
    A sanctuary where all troubles cease
A storm cascades through
    Your bones, each breath, carrying
The weight of loss—whether it's
    the uplift of a cherished moment
Slipping away or the devastation
    Of something irreplaceable
In the midst of that storm a
    Hug becomes a sanctuary, a fragile
Embrace where time holds still
    It is the serenity of surrender
The surrender, the grace of being lost
    In another's warmth, if only
For a fleeting second, a hug speaks
    Where words fall, cradling both
Joy and sorrow, reminding us that
    Even in loss we are not alone

Dana Kay Gregory
Saint Augustine, FL

Amidst devastation—both seen and unseen—a single hug can become a lifeline, offering silent reassurance in the face of overwhelming uncertainty. This poem reflects the weight of what we endure, the unspoken struggles hidden behind resilience, and the profound impact of being held even for a fleeting moment—it speaks to those who long for connection but never ask, to the ones weathering storms alone, inspired by personal longing and the quiet needs of others. This poem is a reminder that sometimes the smallest gesture—a hug— can create a lasting imprint offering refuge in the most unexpected ways.

Index of Poets

Y

Z